Praying  the Psalms

Praying  the Psalms

*Engaging Scripture
and the Life of the Spirit*

Second Edition

WALTER BRUEGGEMANN

Cascade Books
A division of *Wipf & Stock Publishers*
199 West 8th Avenue, Suite 3 • Eugene OR 97401

PRAYING THE PSALMS
Engaging Scripture and the Life of the Spirit
Second Edition

Cascade Books
A Division of Wipf and Stock Publishers
199 W. 8th Ave., Suite 3
Eugene, OR 97401

ISBN 13: 978-1-55635-283-6

Cataloging-in-Publication data:

Brueggemann, Walter.
Praying the Psalms : engaging scripture and the life of the spirit / Walter Brueggemann.

xviii + 98 p.; 20 cm.

Includes bibliographical references.

ISBN 13: 978-1-55635-283-6

1. Bible. O.T. Psalms—Criticism, interpretation, etc. 2. Bible. O.T. Psalms—Devotional Use. 3. Prayer—Biblical Teaching. I. Title.

BS1433 B78 2007

Manufactured in the U.S.A.

for Lila Bonner Miller

Contents

Preface to the First Edition

Psalm study among the scholars has been on something of a plateau for some time. The dominant positions of Hermann Gunkel on form-critical matters and Sigmund Mowinckel on cultic context are still in place. There has been little scholarly movement beyond their brilliant proposals that would link scholarly work to the life of the Psalms in the Church.

But more recently there have been important contributions in developing the connections between scholarship and Church. Among the most important of these are Bernhard Anderson, *Out of the Depths* (Philadelphia: Westminster Press, 1974) and Claus Westermann, *The Psalms: Structure, Content and Message* (Minneapolis: Augsburg Press, 1980). More popularly, see also Thomas H. Troeger, *Rage! Reflect, Rejoice!* (Philadelphia: Westminster Press, 1977). And there is more to come out of the fertile suggestions of Rainer Albertz and Erhard Gerstenberger, whose works await translation.

The present book does not attempt to go over the consensus of scholarship again. Rather than repeat so much material covered in many handbooks, here the work of Gunkel and Mowinckel is assumed. Nor do we need to review the extensive secondary material derived from that consensus. This book attempts to address only two specific issues which hopefully will aid in reading the Psalms both more knowingly and more passionately.

The first issue concerns the function of language in the use of the Psalms. It is clear that conventional exegesis will not make contact with the compelling power of the poetry of the Psalms. And that failure about language in large part is the cause of the gap between the scholarly consensus and the vast array of "devotional materials." I have not spent time here on the foundations of linguistic function to which I appeal. I have tried to show how the Psalms might be liberated for more poignant and faithful use if we will grant the language of the Psalms the imaginative and free play for which it must have been intended. I claim no expertise on linguistic theory. But it will be evident that I have found the work of Paul Ricoeur most helpful and stimulating. A more comprehensive statement of my presuppositions and my utilization of Ricoeur is given in "Psalms and the Life of Faith: A Suggested Typology of Function," *Journal for the Study of the Old Testament* 17 (1980) 3–32.

The second issue considered is the Christian use of poetry which is obviously Jewish. It is clear that the next efforts in Christian theology must concern interaction with Jewish faith. Undoubtedly Jewish faith is problematic for Christians. Concerning the Psalms, Christians (in practice if not in theory) deal with the Jewish "awkwardness" either by cunning selectivity or by knowing spiritualization. Either way, such use misses the point. It is of course hazardous for a Christian to make a statement about the Jewishness in these texts. I have taken a risk about that and perhaps have not done it rightly. But I hope my statement, if it is enough on target, may contribute to the urgent interface of Christian worship and Jewish faith. And even if not right, I hope it is clear that I have acted in good faith.

On both the questions of the liberation of language and Jewish awkwardness, very much is at stake for the Church. I hope to contribute to the vitality of the Church's faith by pointing to the subversive and powerful resources available in the Psalms. It is an unreformed Church which uses the Psalms for a domesticated spirituality. It is not an accident that the Reformers of the sixteenth century attended to the Psalms in intensive ways. On both questions taken up, I have reference to "the one from whom no secret can be hid." On the one hand, I have urged that language here is not only for candor but for the articulation of that which is known both by God and by human persons only when articulated. That is, everything depends on the articulation, for such speech evokes something quite new for both parties in the conversation. That no secret can be hidden depends on such risky articulation.

On the other hand, I have argued that such candor is no empty, neutral form but has a distinctively Jewish shape— the shape of active, protesting suffering; the shape of defiant, resilient hope. The stuff of Jewish suffering and Jewish hope is a unique partner to the form of strident, subversive, intense forms of language. That is, this bold form of speech peculiarly matches the Jewish practice of suffering and hope. It is the interplay of the stuff of Jewish faith and the form of Psalmic speech that might matter to the spirituality of the Church.

I should say a word about how this little book came to be. It is as spotty and selective as it is because it was originally a series of separately printed papers. They were written at the behest of Mary Perkins Ryan, who has had them published in *Professional Approaches for Christian Educators* (PACE) by Saint Mary's Press. The pieces were not intended to be comprehensive or complete; they are only suggestions along the way in reading and praying the Psalms. I have intended that these suggestions should be not only exegetical but hermeneutical as well. Mary Perkins Ryan has been a strong and supportive editor, and I am delighted to express my thanks to her. If these papers do not quite amount to a well-argued book, their original intent and purpose must be kept in mind.

We have determined to include in this publication a copy of the Psalms so that they are immediately available for ready reference as the book is read and studied. We felt the convenience and additional value for the reader definitely warranted the additional cost factor. We have decided to use the Revised Standard Version simply because it probably has the widest usage among readers of the book.

The dedication is to Lila Bonner Miller, M.D. She combines in her life and psychotherapeutic practice all the abrasive candor of liberated faith and all the certitude of unflinching trust that belongs to this tradition. She was formed in the Psalms in the practice of the Associate Reformed Presbyterian Church. Not only has she remained in that nurture—she has practiced the Psalms in bold ways, with both her spirit and her mind (1 Corinthians 14:15). That is a great gift to many persons, including this son-in-law.

Walter Brueggemann
Eden Seminary
Rosh Hashanah (1980 C.E.)

Preface to the Second Edition

I AM DELIGHTED THAT K. C. HANSON HAS taken an initiative to publish a second, somewhat changed, edition of my book, *Praying the Psalms.* Indeed Hanson has not only taken an initiative, but has done the hard work of updating the bibliography and notes for the book, as well as doing careful editing and updating the text of the book itself.

Since the publication of the first edition of the book, I have been constantly involved in the study of and reflection upon the Psalms. Out of my work on the Psalms I have published several volumes: *The Message of the Psalms* (a commentary of selected Psalms), *Psalms and the Life of Faith* (a collection of selected journal articles including my signature essay on "a suggested typology of function"), *Abiding Astonishment* (a study of the so-called "historical Psalms"), and *The Spirituality of the Psalms* (yet another reuse of my essay on typology of function). I am in the final stages of a more complete commentary on the book of Psalms with William Bellinger that will be published in due course by Cambridge University Press.

In the period since the publication of the first edition of the book, a great deal has happened in Old Testament studies. Most specifically, the pretensions of "objective scholarship" have given way to a more candid involvement of the interpreter in the interpretive project. While this has been a hard-won and long-term development in scholarship, the work of Brevard S. Childs is perhaps the epitome of a shifted perspective wherein interpreters are more free and more responsible to read the biblical text "as Scripture." In my own case, as with many other interpreters, the more arid enterprise of genre analysis (a work surely to be continued, but always a step along the way in interpretation) has given way to a thicker reception of the Psalms as acts of faith, acts of worship, and acts of prayer. Out of this awareness, I have published, *Awed to Heaven, Rooted in Earth*, a book of prayers that has grown from my own classroom prayers as a teacher, and *Inscribing the Text*, a collection of prayers and sermons, a collection that has grown from my work as teacher, preacher, and believer. Also in progress is a collection of prayers that will be published by Abingdon Press. I do not imagine that my own leadership of public prayer is more than a modest echo of the Psalms, but then, modesty in such an enterprise is most appropriate. I am also at work on a study of prayers within the text of the Bible that is forthcoming from Westminster John Knox Press.

This shifted focus from "objective" to more passionately confessional work on the Psalms—and if not "confessional" at least "faith-based"—has led my thinking in new theological directions that are personal and immediate for me. I am struck in powerful ways by how the praying voices in the Psalter are passionately *dialogical*. In particular, the evangelical tradition in which I was nurtured rightly taught that prayer is "the conversation of the heart addressed to God," a formula that I believe derives from Augustine. It is a formula that invites honesty, intimacy, deference, and humility—as we are wont to say in my pietistic tradition—"before the throne of mercy."

It took me a long while after my early nurture, however, to sense how deeply interactive the Psalms are, a genuinely two-party enterprise. I suspect that such an interactive sense of the Psalms was inchoate in my theological upbringing; but it required for me to have access to Jewish practices of faith in order to see how deep and insistent is the dialogic interaction of the Psalms. I learned, early on, that the only way to pray dialogically is in a response to the faithfulness and generosity of God who takes all initiatives. I have learned only later, that it is the dialogic courage of laments, complaints, and protests that are crucial to the tradition of the Psalms. In that practice, one is struck by the way in which the Psalms can address demanding imperative to God (which we politely term "petition") without much show of deference. I have concluded that in the dialogic transaction of prayer, there is often a temporary "role reversal" in which Israel takes the lead and holds the upper hand with God, and God is summoned to respond to Israel's urgency in presence and action. That role reversal is temporary, because in due course Israel will praise God in a "return to theological normalcy." Such a return, however, is never to an old comfortable normalcy, for once challenged with venturesome interaction, both parties are, perforce, repositioned in a new relationship.

That repositioning in turn has required a rethinking of the character of God who operates in the Book of Psalms. In my Reformation-Neoorthodox theological education I learned and did know that God takes all important initiatives. But now I am able to see (and hear) that initiative may be taken by either party wherein the addressed party (Israel or God) is summoned to respond and "obey." Such an articulation of the transaction means that the character of God is taken to be supple and open, exposed to risk and placed in jeopardy by the urgency of Israel. Such risk and jeopardy may be only momentary, after which things "settle" again; in that moment, however, God is shown to be a full participant in a life of lively dialogue.

Mutatis mutandis, such a dialogic exchange rearticulates Israel as well—or a praying Israelite or any of us who pray who follow in the way of Israel—as a partner in dialogue who is capable of being an *initiator* or a *respondent* in such exchange, and therefore regularly exposed to summons, risk, and jeopardy.

The outcome of such insistent utterance has been important to me in my practice of prayer and in the fuller scope of my continuing study of these texts of prayer. I have come to understand, in ways that have been an enormous challenge to me, the dialogical quality of faith that leaves our life with God always open and unsettled, and available for new demanding/yielding venture.

Since my study of and life in prayer is never far removed from my attempt to live in the world, I have been able to see from the dialogic interaction of prayer, that this permit for dialogue becomes a model for a dialogic life in the world wherein, when we have courage, truth may speak to power. This has become a pivot point in my social analysis as I have seen clearly how our common social life is deeply tilted toward monologue, a one-way mode of "power and truth" by large concentrations of economic and political power, by an oligarchic government that refuses dialogue through the steady work of ideology, propaganda, advertising and a combination of manipulation and muscle. That mode of monologue, moreover, is often imitated in the life of the church where truth comes along with power, and in interpersonal relations where power is always operative. In the face of these lethal reductionisms in our common life, the practice of a dialogic life—with God and with neighbor—is, whenever it occurs, an important act of subversion.

All of this, of course, is very Jewish. It is reflective of Martin Buber's "I-Thou" and Emmanuel Levinas's "face-to-faceness." I have thought sometimes that even Levinas (and even more Buber), in their articulation of the human "I" before the divine "Thou," have been too restrained, too deferential, and too polite. That judgment is simply a recognition that the Psalms, in their boldness and passion, are out beyond our conventional liturgical and devotional practices. We are always hurrying to catch up with the daring faith of the Psalter. When we catch up with it here and there, now and then, the transaction itself, in its transformative force, is nothing less than resurrection, the gift of new life that the God praised and summoned intends us to have. I am still under way with these matters, and am grateful for the chance I have to stand regularly—with good companions—before these texts and before the God who meets us therein.

As a teacher I have come to see that my responsibility is to evoke honest, passionate, serious dialogue in the pedagogical process. Thus I am even more convinced that *face-to-faceness* with text and with tradition matter decisively for the emancipatory experience that is the heart of education. Such a conviction causes me to be very nervous about the triumph of the technological in education, even in theological education. That may be no more than my old-fashionedness, or it may be a claim deep in the tradition. It is too soon to say; but better to think about it before it is too late. If the teaching-learning enterprise is thus *face to face dialogue*, then such a model for instruction grows out of prayer, the primal instance of such engagement inescapably filled with risk and with possibility.

Walter Brueggemann

March 30, 2007

1

Letting Experience Touch the Psalter

We pray together regularly "for all sorts and conditions of men" (and women), as the *Book of Common Prayer* puts it.[1] We know all about those sorts and conditions, for we are among and like all those others. When we pray for all those others, we pray for ourselves along with them. We are able to pray for the others precisely because we share a "common lot." They are like us and we are like them in decisive ways. Thus one way of knowing about "all sorts and conditions of men" and women is to be attentive to what is happening in our own lives.

A second way in which we know about those others is to be attentive to what is written—in the daily newspaper as well as in great literature. The daily newspaper is a summary and chronicle of what goes on among us, the healings and betrayals, the reality of power sought and gained, of brokenness and gifts and victories. All of that belongs to these "sorts and conditions" for whom we pray.

In addition to our own experience and the testimonies of print, the Psalms of the Old Testament offer a third presentation of how it is with all sorts and conditions of men and women. The Psalms, with a few exceptions, are not the voice of God addressing us. They are rather the voice of our own

1. *The Book of Common Prayer*, 355.

common humanity—gathered over a long period of time, but a voice that continues to have amazing authenticity and contemporaneity. It speaks about life the way it really is, for in those deeply human dimensions the same issues and possibilities persist. And so when we turn to the Psalms it means we enter into the midst of that voice of humanity and decide to take our stand with that voice. We are prepared to speak among them and with them and for them, to express our solidarity in this anguished, joyous human pilgrimage. We add a voice to the common elation, shared grief, and communal rage that besets us all.

In order to pray the Psalms, our work (liturgy is indeed work) is to let our voices and minds and hearts run back and forth in regular and speedy interplay between the stylized and sometimes too familiar words of Scripture and our experience which we sense with poignancy. And when we do, we shall find that the words of Scripture bring power, shape, and authority to what we know about ourselves. Conversely, our experience will bring to the words of Scripture a vitality and immediacy that must always be reasserted within the Psalter.

Beyond Our Time of Equilibrium

Before turning to the Psalms, let us consider what are those "sorts and conditions" which are true of all of us and which come to speech in the Psalms. I suggest, in a simple schematic fashion, that our life of faith consists in moving with God in terms of:

    (a) being securely oriented;
    (b) being painfully disoriented; and
    (c) being surprisingly reoriented.

This general way of speaking can apply to our self-acceptance, our relations to significant others, our participation in public issues. It can permit us to speak of "passages," the life-cycle, stages of growth, and identity crises. It can permit us to be honest about what is happening to us. Most of all, it may provide us a way to think about the Psalms in relation to our common human experience, for each of God's children is in transit along the flow of orientation, disorientation, and reorientation.

The first situation in this scheme, that of being securely oriented, is a situation of equilibrium. While we all yearn for it, it is not very interesting and it does not produce great prayer or powerful song. It consists in being well-settled, knowing that life makes sense and God is well-placed in heaven, presiding but not bothering. This is the mood of much of the middle-class Church. In terms of the Bible, this attitude of equilibrium and safe orientation is best reflected in the teaching of the ancient book of Proverbs which affirms that life is equitable, symmetrical, and well-proportioned. This mood of humanness is minimal in the Psalms but may be reflected in Psalm 37, which is mostly a collection of sayings that could as well be placed in Proverbs. And the same is more eloquently reflected in such a marvelous statement as Psalm 145, which trusts everything to God. Such Psalms reflect confident well-being.[2] In order to pray them, we must locate either in our

2. Note that Psalms 37 and 145 are both alphabetic acrostic poems. Each full line (145) or every other line (37) begins with the sequential letters of the Hebrew alphabet—thus reflecting the "orderliness" and "symmetry" of the poems' contents. See also Psalms 9–10; 25; 34; 111; 112; 119; Proverbs 31:10–31; Lamentations 1–4; Nahum 1; and Sirach 51:13–30; as well as Psalm 155 and the Apostrophe of Zion from the Dead Sea Scrolls.

lives or in the lives of others situations of such confident, buoyant, "successful" living.

But that is a minor theme in the Psalms and not very provocative. The Psalms mostly do not emerge out of such situations of equilibrium. Rather, people are driven to such poignant prayer and song as are found in the Psalter precisely by experiences of dislocation and relocation. It is experiences of being overwhelmed, nearly destroyed, and surprisingly given life that empower us to pray and sing.

In the Rawness of Life

Recently there has been considerable discussion of those events which drive us to the edge of humanness and make us peculiarly open to the Holy One. This investigation, pertinent to our theme, is undertaken because many persons conclude that the "religious dimension" of their life is void. And so there is an asking about those elements in our life that relate to the "hunger for transcendence." In a variety of ways, it is suggested that the events at the edge of our humanness—the ones that threaten and disrupt our convenient equilibrium—are the events that may fill us with passion and evoke in us eloquence. Thus the Psalms mostly reflect such events of passion and eloquence when we are pressed by experience to address the Holy One.

We have noted the convergence of: (a) our experience, (b) the account of the newspaper, and (c) the Psalms as being articulations of our deep human experience. But we should distinguish the Psalms in one important point as being different. Unlike our own experience and that of the newspaper, it is the Psalms that present "all sorts and conditions of men" and women addressed to the Holy God. Thus the events at the edge of humanness which are so crucial for us and that are reflected in the Psalms tend to: evoke eloquence, fill us with passion, and turn us to the Holy One. As we enter into the prayer and song of common humanity in the Psalms, it is helpful to be attentive precisely to the simple eloquence, the overriding passion, and the bold ways in which this voice turns to the Holy One.

And what situations drive us to the edge of our humanness? They are situations of extremity for which conventional equilibrium offers no adequate base. Peter Berger refers to these extremities as experiences that are filled with "rumors of angels," that is, hints of some surplus of meaning. He suggests they include experiences of order, play, hope, damnation, and humor.[3]

Langdon Gilkey speaks of experiences of "contingency" when we become aware of how precarious our life is and aware also of the inexplicable givenness of it.[4] For him, these dimensions include experiences of givenness, threat, limitedness, value, freedom, and condemnation. Paul Ricoeur refers to "limit-experiences." Following Karl Jaspers, he includes death, suffering, guilt, and hatred; but they may also include "'peak experiences,' especially experiences of creation and joy which are no less extreme than are experiences of catastrophe."[5] These articulations by Berger, Gilkey, and Ricoeur tell us something important about prayer, especially in the Psalms. Reflect for a moment on the coined phrases of "rumor of angels," "the

---

3. Berger, *A Rumor of Angels.*
4. Gilkey, *Naming the Whirlwind.*
5. Ricoeur, "Biblical Hermeneutics," 34.

whirlwind," "contingency" "limit-experiences." In different ways, all these writers—a sociologist, a theologian, and a philosopher interested in psychology—all of them are pointing to the deep discontinuities in our lives where most of us live, on which we use most of our energies, and about which we are regularly preoccupied.

Thus we follow them in suggesting that it is the experiences of life that lie beyond our conventional copings that make us eloquent and passionate and that drive us to address ourselves to the Holy One. And it is experiences beyond conventional orientations that come to vivid expression in the Psalms. That is what we mean by "all sorts and conditions of men" and women—that we have to do here with the powerful, dangerous, and joyful rawness of human reality. And in the Psalms, we find the voice that dares to speak of these matters with eloquence and passion to the Holy One. Psalms offer speech when life has gone beyond our frail efforts to control.

Anticipating Ricoeur in important ways, Karl Barth wrote:

> It is no accident that of all the books of the Old Testament the Psalter has always been found the most relevant. This is not in spite of the fact, but just because of it, that in so many passages it echoes the people of the covenant trembling for its preservation in final extremity before its all-powerful enemies. The Christian community always has good reason to see itself in this people, and to take on its own lips the words of its helpless sighing, the cries which it utters from the depths of its need. It turns to the Psalter, not in spite of the fact, but just because of it, that as the community of Jesus Christ it knows that it is established on the rock (as power-

fully attested by the Psalms themselves), but on the rock which, although it is sure and impregnable in itself, is attacked on all sides, and seems to be of very doubtful security in the eyes of all men and therefore in its own.[6]

Note that the Psalms thus propose to speak about human experience in an honest, freeing way. This is in contrast to much human speech and conduct which is in fact a cover-up. In most arenas where people live, we are expected and required to speak the language of safe orientation and equilib-rium, either to find it so or to pretend we find it so. For the normal, conventional functioning of public life, the raw edges of disorientation and reorientation must be denied or sup-pressed for purposes of public equilibrium. As a result, our speech is dulled and mundane. Our passion has been stilled and is without imagination. And mostly the Holy One is not addressed —not because we dare not, but because God is far away and hardly seems important. This means that the agenda and intention of the Psalms is considerably at odds with the normal speech of most people, the normal speech of a stable, functioning, self-deceptive culture in which everything must be kept running young and smooth.

Against that, the speech of the Psalms is abrasive, revo-lutionary, and dangerous. It announces that life is not like that, that our common experience is not one of well-being and equilibrium, but a churning, disruptive experience of disloca-tion and relocation. Perhaps in our conventional, routinized prayer life (for example, the daily practice of the office) that is one of the reasons the Psalter does not yield its power—be-

6. Barth, *Church Dogmatics* IV.2, 671.

cause out of habit or fatigue or numbness, we try to use the Psalms in our equilibrium. And when we do that, we miss the point of the Psalms. Moreover, our own experience may be left untapped and inarticulate and therefore not liberated. Such surface use of the Psalms coincides with the denial of the discontinuities in our own experience. Ernest Becker has written of "the denial of death."[7] By "the denial of death" Becker refers to the given limit of human reality and the refusal to accept that horizon of mortality. That refusal is evidenced in both the endless attempts to outflank the diminishment of our bodies (diet, exercise, cosmetics) and in the lethal ordering of the body politic in a frantic attempt to maintain control over a life that cannot finally be controlled. But such denial happens not just at the crisis points. It happens daily in the reduction of language to numb conventions.

Thus I suggest that most of the Psalms can only be appropriately prayed by people who are living at the edge of their lives, sensitive to the raw hurts, the primitive passions, and the naïve elations that are at the bottom of our life. For most of us, liturgical or devotional entry into the Psalms requires a real change of pace. It asks us to depart from the closely managed world of public survival, to move into the open, frightening, healing world of speech with the Holy One.

Complaint as Speeches of Disorientation

So let us consider in turn the experiences of disorientation and reorientation that characterize human life and that are the driving power of the Psalms. If we move from the premise of equilibrium, we may speak of chaos (disorder) and new

7. Becker, *The Denial of Death*.

order. And these are elemental dimensions, both to our experience and to the Psalms. The Psalms, by and large, emerge from and reflect precisely such situations of chaos and new order. And any attempt to take these speech-events of chaos and new order and make them instruments of conventional equilibrium is a travesty. To make the Psalms serve "business as usual" misunderstands the Psalms, even though habitual use of them has tended to do just that.

So first, the reality of chaos, disorder, disorientation. Each of us knows about that in our own life. It may be a visible issue like a marriage failure, the loss of job, a financial reverse, the diagnosis of the doctor. Or it may be nothing more than a cross word, a disappointing letter, a sharp criticism, a minor illness. Or it may be disturbance of a public kind, anxiety over the loss of energy, revulsion at the sickening spectacle of war, the sense that the world is falling apart before our very eyes, the unspeakable horror of a possible nuclear war. It may be the discovery of loneliness or the sense of being rejected and unloved. All—or any—of these is the awareness that life is not whole, that it is not the romantic well-being that we may have been comforted with as children and that is so shamefully and shrewdly reflected in television ads. Indeed the world is a dangerous, frightening place, and I am upset for myself. And when I can move beyond my own fear and grief, I do not need to look far to find the hurt and terror in others, whether these others are my own friends or people I see and hear about in the media.

The Psalter knows that life is dislocated. No cover-up is necessary. The Psalter is a collection over a long period of time of the eloquent, passionate songs and prayers of people who are at the desperate edge of their lives. The stylized form of such speech is the complaint or supplication psalm, of which there are many examples in the Psalter. The best known is Psalm 22 ("My God, my God, why have you forsaken me?"). The neatest, simplest example is Psalm 13. The angriest, most hopeless is Psalm 88, which ends in unreserved, unrelieved gloom:

> Your anger has swept over me;
>> your dread assaults destroy me.
> They surround me like a flood throughout the day;
>> from all sides they close in on me.
> You have caused friend and neighbor to shun me;
>> my companions are in darkness." (Psalm 88:16–18)

Thus I propose a direct link between the experience of dislocation in which we all share and the complaint psalm of Israel. There are those who know about disorientation but have no speech which can adequately say it. But there are also those (and this is our primary concern here) who face the complaint psalm but do not bring to it the raw disorientation that is all about us and that is the intended agenda of the psalm. It is the work of the one who prays a psalm to be actively engaged in holding this linkage in a conscious, concrete way. For when we do, we discover that this psalm is affected by our experience. And even more surprising, we find that our experience has been dealt with by the psalm.

We must not make these Psalms too "religious" or pious. Most of the complaint psalms are the voice of those who say "We are mad as hell, and we are not going to take it any more," as the character Howard Beal says in the movie *Network*. They are not religious in the sense that they are courteous or polite or deferential. They are religious only in the sense that they are willing to articulate this chaos to the very face of the Holy One. Thus the complaint psalm, for all its preoccupation with the hard issue at hand, invariably calls God by name and expects a response. At this crucial point, the psalm parts company with our media evidence and most of our experience, for it is disorientation addressed to God. And in that address, something happens to the disorientation.

The Surprising Songs of Newness

The other movement of human life is the surprising move from disorientation to a new orientation that is quite unlike the old status quo. This is not an automatic movement that can be presumed upon or predicted. Nor is it a return to the old form, a return to normalcy as though nothing had happened. It is rather "all things new." And when it happens, it is always a surprise, always a gift of graciousness, and always an experience that evokes gratitude. It may be thought that in our daily experience the events of reorientation are not as frequent as are the times of dislocation. Perhaps that is so. Perhaps we have not learned to discern the ways the wondrous gift is given. We dare to say that in our existence there is the richness of life along with the reality of death. We experience the power of resurrection as well as the inescapability of crucifixion. The conquest of chaos and the gift of fresh life-giving order must also be brought to speech. Such experiences include all those gifts of friendship and caring, all those gestures of reconciliation and forgiveness, all those risky signs of hope in public life: the initiative of Egyptian President Anwar Sadat to go to Jerusalem, the bold women in Ireland who march for peace, the great festivals of reconciliation in the Church. In recent time we have witnessed the fall of the Soviet Union with its coercive governance, the end of apartheid in South Africa, and more recently attestation to the gift of God's reconciling order is evident in the new "unity government" in Northern Ireland brokered by Ian Paisley and Gerry Adams. There are, of course, many less well known wondrous gifts of God's new order in local settings, for example that The Church of the Savior (Washington, DC) daily receives seventy or so newly released prisoners into its welcoming presence. It is not possible for the faithful to view these astonishing turns in human history apart from the working of God's governance. All these experiences may touch us deeply and announce that God has not left the world to chaos (cf. Isaiah 45:18–19).

These events we may not notice unless we practice the language of praise and thanks. And for this, the Psalter offers us the celebrative language of hymns and songs of thanksgiving, which sometimes assert the abiding rule of God, as in Psalm 103:

> Bless Yahweh, O my soul,
>> and all that is within me his holy name.
> Bless Yahweh, O my soul,
>> and do not forget any of his benefits. (vv. 1–2)

But at other times it announces the surprising intrusion of God who just now makes things good,[8] for example Psalm 30:

---

8. On the cruciality of thanksgiving for the faith and worship of Israel, see the fine discussion by Guthrie, *Theology as Thanksgiving*; and idem, *Israel's Sacred Songs*, 147–57.

> I will exalt you, O Yahweh, for you have pulled me up,
>> and you did not allow my enemies to rejoice over me.
> O Yahweh, my God, I cried out to you for help,
>> and you have healed me. (vv. 1–2)

That is what is meant in those psalms that announce that "God is King," for example:

> Proclaim to the foreigners:
>> "Yahweh is king!"
> The world is firmly established;
>> It shall never be moved.
> He will rule the peoples with equity. (Psalm 96:10)

> Yahweh is king! Let the earth rejoice!
>> Let the many coastlands by glad! (Psalm 97:1)

> Yahweh is king!
>> Let the peoples tremble!
> He sits enthroned between the cherubim!
>> Let the earth quake! (Psalm 99:1)

They celebrate some experience that has brought the world to a new joyous orientation that is experienced by the speaker. Thus I suggest that there is a linkage to be maintained between the experiences of reorientation and Israel's psalms of thanksgiving and hymns. There are those who have a sense of the new gift of life and lamentably have no way to speak about it. But there are also those (and this is our primary concern here) who have regular access to the psalms of high celebration but have been so numbed to their own experience that the words of the psalm have no counterpart in their own life experience.

The collection of the Psalter is not for those whose life is one of uninterrupted continuity and equilibrium. Such people should stay safely in the book of Proverbs, which reflects on the continuities of life. But few of us live that kind of life. Most of us who think our lives are that way have been numbed, desensitized, and suppressed so that we are cut off from what is in fact going on in our lives.

The Psalms are an assurance to us that when we pray and worship, we are not expected to censure or deny the deepness of our own human pilgrimage. Rather, we are expected to submit it openly and trustingly so that it can be brought to eloquent and passionate speech addressed to the Holy One. If we are genuinely attentive to these linkages of speech and experience, we will discover that we pray a prayer along with our brothers and sisters in very different circumstances. Others may give a different nuance to their speech, but they also have the realities of disorientation and reorientation in their lives. And they thus join in this resilient voice addressed to the Holy One.

It is clear that those who pray for and witness to God's newness never do so alone. While there are (thank God!) spectacular individual persons who receive headlines for their courage, such individual persons are invariably evoked and sustained by communal affirmation. Thus Martin Luther King Jr. was situated in a vibrant African-American Church. Daniel Berrigan is clearly the product of the Eucharistic community to which he belonged from his earliest time in family. In the ancient Psalms and in current usage, the saints are always participants in "the communion of saints." Otherwise boldness could not be sustained but would quickly eventuate in cynicism or despair.

The Psalms are not used in a vacuum, but in a history where we are dying and rising, and in a history where God is at work, ending our lives and making gracious new beginnings for us. The Psalms move with our experience. They may also take us beyond our own guarded experience into the more poignant pilgrimages of sisters and brothers.

2

The Liberation of Language

PRAYING THE PSALMS DEPENDS UPON TWO things: (1) what we find when we come to the Psalms that is already there; and (2) what we bring to the Psalms out of our own lives. In chapter 1, I have urged that when we come to the Psalms we shall find their eloquence and passion and boldness in addressing the Holy One. Further, I have urged that what we bring to the Psalter in order to pray is a candid openness to the extremities in our own lives and in the lives of others, extremities that recognize the depths of despair and death, that acknowledge the sheer gift of life.

The work of prayer is to bring these two realities together—the boldness of the Psalms and the extremity of our experience—to let them interact, play with each other, tease each other, and illuminate each other. The work of prayer consists in the imaginative use of language to give the extremities their full due and to force new awareness and new configurations of reality by the boldness of our speech. All this is to submit to the Holy One in order that we may be addressed by a Word that out-distances all our speech.

A Language Adequate to Experience

Let us begin with a presupposition about language that is necessary to entering into the Psalms. In our culture, we imbibe a positivistic understanding of language. That is, we believe that the function of language is only to report and describe what already exists. The usefulness of such language is obvious. It lets us be precise and unambiguous. It even lets us control. But it is one-dimensional language that must necessarily be without passion and without eloquence and indeed without boldness. It is useful language, but it is not the language we have in the Psalms. Indeed it is not the language in which we can faithfully pray. Such language is useful for managing things. But it makes no impact on how things really are, for things would be the same even if there were no such speech.

By contrast, in the Psalms the use of language does not describe what is. It evokes into being what does not exist until it has been spoken. This kind of speech resists discipline, shuns precision, delights in ambiguity, is profoundly creative, and is itself an exercise in freedom. In using speech in this way, we are in fact doing in a derivative way what God has done in the creation narratives of Genesis. We are calling into being that which does not yet exist (compare Romans 4:17).

Now in contrasting these two kinds of language, we need to be clear about the social function of each. The first mode of language—appropriate to science, engineering, and perhaps the social sciences—when used in the arena of human interaction, tends to be conservative, restrictive, limiting. It can only describe what already exists and, by its very use, deter anything new from coming into being. It crushes hope, for it cannot "imagine" what is not already present. By contrast, the bold, symbolic use of language in the Psalms is restive with what is. It races on ahead to form something new that never was before. This language then, with its speech of liberation, is dangerous and revolutionary, for its very use constitutes a threat to the way things have been. It is for that reason that totalitarian regimes, even when they control all the hardware, are most fearful of the poet. The creative speech of the poet can evoke new forms of human life which even the power of arms and repression is helpless to prevent. Such speech, which is the proper idiom for prayer, is the language of surprise. It means that in such speech both the speaker and God may be surprised by what is freshly offered. The language of the Psalms permits us to be boldly anticipatory about what may be, as well as discerning about what has been.

A great danger in praying the Psalms is that we shall mistakenly take their language in a positivistic, descriptive way as nothing more than a report on what is. Taken that way, the Psalms can probably be managed and comprehended and rendered powerless. That is a hazard of the repeated use of any important words. We assume we already know what they mean. But if the language of the Psalms is understood impressionistically and creatively, then it holds surprise and in fact creates new realities where none existed before.

Complaint as Candor and Anticipation

Let us consider the function and power of such speech with reference to the two kinds of psalms we identified in chapter 1. First, we said that psalms of complaint are powerful expressions of the experience of disorientation. They express the pain, grief, dismay, and anger that life is not good. (They also refuse to settle for things as they are, and so they assert hope.) One of the things to notice is that these Psalms engage in enormous hyperbole. Thus:

I am poured out like water,
    all my bones are out of joint;
my heart is like wax;
    it is melted within my chest;
my strength is dried up like a potsherd,
    and my tongue sticks to my jaws;
    you lay me in the dust of death. (Psalm 22:14–15)

Every night I flood my bed with tears,
    I drench my couch with my weeping. (Psalm 6:6)

My tears have been my food day and night.
(Psalm 42:3; cf. Isaiah 16:9)

My enemies trample upon me all the day long.
(Psalm 56:1)

I lie in the midst of lions. (Psalm 57:4)

What are we to make of this? If this be descriptive speech, we may take it as likely that not every bone is out of joint, that not the whole bed is drenched, that there must have been other meat, that the speaker has not been trampled all day, for that happens only in TV wrestling. Or if it is descriptive, we must conclude that the speech is irrelevant, because it resembles no experience of our own. But this is not descriptive language. It is evocative language used to create between speaker and God something that did not fully exist before, namely, a total, publicly acknowledged event of dislocation and disorientation. With this speech, the dislocation becomes a visible event that now exists between the pray-er and God. With this portrayal, God is compelled to notice. We now know, of course, that at the time of death, the healthy grief process requires many tears, many words, many embraces, many retellings of the grief. It is so for every extremity of dislocation. This is indeed grief work and we are invited to join in it.

The function of such complaint speech is to create a situation that did not exist before the speech, to create an external event that matches the internal sensitivities. It is the work of such speech to give shape, power, visibility, authenticity to the experience. The speaker now says, "It is really like that. That is my situation." The listener knows, "Now I understand fully your actual situation in which you are at work dying to the old equilibrium that is slipping from you." The language may even run ahead of the event. Ricoeur (to whom much of this discussion is indebted), following Freud, has seen that the authentic artist is not focusing on old events for review (after the manner of the analyst) but is in fact committing an act of hope.[1] Art therapists know that persons who draw and paint are not simply announcing the old death but are choosing a future they are yet to embrace. Thus the complaint psalms of disorientation do their work of helping people to die completely to the old situation, the old possibility, the old false hopes, the old lines of defense and pretense, to say as dramatically as possible, "That is all over now."

When we hear someone speak desperately about a situation, our wont is to rush in and reassure that it is not all that bad. And in hearing these Psalms, our natural, fearful yearning is to tone down the hyperbole, to deny it for ourselves and protect others from it because it is too harsh and, in any case,

1. Ricoeur, *Freud and Philosophy,* 165–77. Ricoeur increasingly seeks a hermeneutic of anticipation, which draws his work into relation with that of Jürgen Habermas.

is an overstatement. And likely we wish to hold on a bit to the old orientation now in such disarray. Our tendency to such protectiveness is evident in the way churches ignore or "edit" these "unacceptable" Psalms.

Our retreat from the poignant language of such a Psalm is in fact a denial of the disorientation and a yearning to hold on to the old orientation that is in reality dead. Thus an evangelical understanding of reality affirms that the old is passing away, that God is bringing in a newness (2 Corinthians 5:17). But we know also that there is no newness unless and until there is a serious death of the old (see John 12:25 and 1 Corinthians 15:36). Thus the complaint psalms of disorientation can be understood, not in a theoretical but in a quite concrete way as an act of putting off the old humanity that the new may come (see Ephesians 4:22–24).

So how shall we pray these psalms? I suggest that praying them requires the location of experiences in our own lives and in the lives of others, when such inclinations and realities of disorientations were singing among us. The events of a bed full of tears, of a body full of disconnectedness, of a plate full of salty tears, of a day full of trampling—these are events not remote from us. In our disciplined, restrained ways of managing, we may be too uptight to cry so. We may be too dulled to feel the trampling or to acknowledge it. But we do know what it feels like to be kicked when we are down. How wondrous that these Psalms make it clear that precisely such dimensions of our life are the stuff of prayer. The Psalms thus become a voice for the dying in which we are all engaged, partly because the world is a place of death and is passing away, partly because God gives new life, but only in the pain of death. It is because God is at work even in the pain of such death that the Psalmist dares enter God's presence with these realities. They have to do with God.

Language Permitting Transformation

The celebrative psalms of thanksgiving and hymns powerfully express experiences of reorientation. The reorientation is always a surprise and a gift. It always comes to us just when we thought it not possible, when we could not see how it could be wrought in the present circumstance. The reorientation is not an achievement coming from us. It is not an automatic "next stage" ordained in our body, but it is something we receive when we did not expect it at all. Life falls into patterns of wholeness where we did not think it could happen precisely and only because God is at work.

Again we shall see that the psalms of celebration also greatly overstate the case because they are essentially promissory. That is, they are not descriptions of what is evident, but they are renderings of what is surely promised and toward which the speaker is prepared to live. It may be urged, here more than in the psalms of complaint, that these statements engage in fantasy and assert things that are not "in hand." Thus, for example, the key assertion of these psalms, "Yahweh is king," strikes one as ludicrous in our world, because most of the evidence of the newspapers suggests God is not in power. If the words must be descriptive, then such a claim is deceptive, for God manifestly is not king. But if the words are evocative of a new reality yet to come to being, then the words have a powerful function. And indeed, sometimes in a world where the circumstances are hopeless, then a promissory word is all that stands between us and the chaos. Then it is important to pray and speak and sing and share that word against all that data. For such a word stands like a barrier thrown up against the sea (see Jeremiah 5:22). And we do know that in our most precious friendships, sometimes there is only a word between us and misery, between us and death. But that word is not a fantasy. It is, rather, a precious gift on which we will stake everything. Thus as the psalms of complaint are acts of painful relinquishment,[2] so celebrative psalms are acts of radical hope.

In the Psalms of celebration, we may consider three ways of speaking which correlate to those we have cited in the complaints.

First, songs of complaint focus frequently on the threat of enemies seeking to destroy. Many of these Psalms speak about enemies, even though they are not clearly identified. The responding assertion of celebration is that Yahweh is king, that God is graciously inclined and powerfully enthroned and that because of his rule, the enemies are no threat. Most scholars agree that at least in Psalms 47, 93, 96–99 this is the central motif. In a less precise way, this is a main theme of every song of celebration: the triumphant rule of Yahweh against every agent who would diminish us. Those who pray this kind of Psalm will want not just to reflect on a general notion of well-being but to work with the concrete image of king, the gracious ruler who does indeed manage well, provide for, protect the weak, and intervene for the helpless. To provide concreteness, it may be useful to focus in our own

2. On the complaint as the route to hope, see Gerstenberger, "Der klagende Mensch"; idem, "Life Situations and Theological Concepts of Old Testament Psalms"; and Brueggemann, "The Formfulness of Grief."

lives on situations when the presence of a trusted, respected person made a decisive difference, simply by being present. Or one may wish to reflect on the times of intervention when the kingship of Jesus totally redefined a situation (see Mark 3:1–6; 5:15, 41–42; 6:41–44).

Second, we have commented on the diet of tears that belongs to the complaint. In the songs of celebration, the metaphor of tears is perhaps balanced by the metaphor of food, of banquet, of a bounteous table. Of course, the best known of these is in Psalm 23:5, "You prepare a table before me in the presence of my enemies." For a terser style, see Psalm 146:7:

> who executes justice for the oppressed;
> who gives food to the hungry.

And Psalm 147:9 depicts Yahweh as the provider of food to the other creatures of the earth (see also Psalm 81:10).

An engagement of the metaphor of food is fundamental. There is no gesture as expressive of utter well-being as lavish food—as every Jewish and every Christian mother knows. Thus the feeding miracles of Jesus and the Eucharist are gestures of a new orientation that comes as surprising gift and ends all diets of tears.

Third, we have considered the metaphor of being trampled as a motif of disorientation. Notice that in being trampled, one is passive and acted upon. I suggest that in the songs of celebration, perhaps a counterpart of being trampled on is the act of clapping, of actively publicly engaging in a concrete gesture of commitment and reception of the new time. The clapping is to cheer the new king, that is, the new orientation, the arrival of the promised kingdom:

> Clap your hand, all you peoples;
>> shout to God with loud songs of joy!
> (Psalms 47:1; 98:8; see Isaiah 55:12)

Less concrete, but related to it, is the call to praise; so that in the later Psalms—especially Psalm 148 (see also 149:1–3, 5–6)—everything and everyone is mobilized to applaud, welcome, and receive.

> Praise Yahweh! Praise Yahweh from the heavens;
>> praise him on the heights!
> Praise him, all his angels;
>> Praise him, all his army!
>
> Praise him, sun and moon!
>> Praise him, all you shimmering stars!
> Praise him, you highest heavens,
>> and you waters above the heavens! (Psalm 148:1–4)

In praying these psalms, the one who prays may want to recall times in which there was some good news which had to be shared. Other people had to be recruited to celebrate and rejoice because the news was too good to keep to one's self (see Luke 15:6, 9, 23).

Poetry Requiring Work

So let me conclude this with three comments. First, I have urged that the Psalms are filled with metaphors that need to be accepted as metaphors and not flattened into descriptive words. Metaphors are quite concrete words rooted in visible reality but yet are enormously elastic, giving full play to imagination in stretching and extending far beyond the concrete referent to touch all kinds of experience. The meaning of the metaphor is determined not only by what is there but by what we bring to it out of our experience and out of our imagination.

The work of prayer is fully to explore and exploit the metaphor in terms of our own experience. Thus "table" does not mean simply what the speaker in Psalm 23 means, but it means all the good tables at which you have ever sat and the experiences of joy that happened there and the subsequent vibrations you have from them. "Tears night and day" does not refer simply to the crying a particular psalmist did, but to all the times of crying in which you have engaged the death of the old world and all the times you have needed to cry but were unable to, all the bitterness and rejection that both caused crying and prevented it. All that is to be brought to the metaphor. Metaphors are not packaged announcements; they are receptive vehicles waiting for a whole world of experience that is itself waiting to come to expression. And if, in the praying of the Psalms, we do not bring the dynamic of our own experience, we shall have flat, empty prayers treating the language as one-dimensional description.

Second, this exposition assumes something about how we read and study and hear these materials. The Psalms do not insist that we follow word-for-word and line-by-line, but they intend us to have great freedom to engage our imagination toward the Holy God. Our listening mostly moves in and out by a free association of ideas. Whether we plan it or not, are permitted or not, we will take liberties as the psalm passes by to move out into the richness of our experience and then back into the awesome presence of God. That is the way of metaphors. They are not aisles down which we must move;

they are more like rockets that explode in ways we cannot predict, causing some things to become unglued and creating new configurations of sensitivity. Like other rockets, if we are attentive they may both shatter and illuminate. The Psalms are our partners in prayer. Such evocative language permits both partners a marvelous freedom with which to surprise the other.

Third, I have offered three pairs of metaphors that I suggest can be useful in bringing experience to the Psalms:

enemies who destroy / king who orders and governs
being trampled / clapping
tears / table.

The first element of each pair comes from the complaints. The speech and experience of disorientation is a sense of being gotten at and trampled, which reduces to tears. The second triad is for celebration: of having a sense of all-rightness, of needing to dramatize it, and of knowing nourishment. With such a simple scheme, many of the Psalms are embraced and much of our experience is submitted.

The images and metaphors I have suggested are rather at random. The Psalms are rich with others. And if these are not the ones that permit linkage for you, it will be easy enough to find others. If we do our proper work, we discover that these poetic pilgrimages are indeed ones with God "from whom no secret can be hid." In any case, this kind of language is not flat, obvious, or easy. It is language that requires us to work to bring something to it of our experience. But it also gives freedom. And when we speak this way, we are surprised by gifts given and lives raised from death.

3
Language
Appropriate to a Place

✳ In chapter 2, I referred to "the liberation of language." That is the theme we intend to pursue here. It is our argument that the linkage between the Psalms and our experience requires understanding of and being attentive to language. The movement and meeting of God with us is indeed a speech-event in which new humanness is evoked among us. Being attentive to language means cultivating the candid imagination to bring our own experience to the Psalms and permitting it to be disciplined by the speech of the Psalms. And, conversely, it means letting the Psalms address us and having that language reshape our sensitivities and fill our minds with new pictures and images that may redirect our lives.

The notion of the "liberation of language" cuts two ways. On the one hand, we may be more free with our language, to let our language be liberated—not by being permissive or vulgar, but by letting it move beyond descriptive functions to evocative, creative functions in our life. That language should be free means we will turn it loose to form new possibilities for us, allowing us to engage in speech that is hope-filled.

On the other hand, the notion of the liberation of language is not only about free speech, but about speech freeing us. Thus we may become aware that when speech is broken free from a need for exactitude and permitted to reshape our existence and experience, we will experience new freedom that is not just freedom of speech, but freedom for faith. Language matters enormously. If our speech and the speech of the Bible must be too closely managed, it likely means restriction both of God and us. On the other hand, free speech for God may release the energy which leads to "all things new."

The psalmic metaphors we consider offer to us not descriptions but news, not situations but movements of God that will change things. Praying the Psalms means openness to God's pilgrimage toward us.

Our work in praying the Psalms is somehow to bring the stylized, disciplined speech of the Psalms together with the raw, ragged, mostly formless experience in our lives. We have suggested that a way to do this is by exploration and exploitation of metaphors, that is, words that have concrete reference but which are open to remarkable stretching in many directions in order to touch our experience. The liberation of language means, then, that these words are free to work in many directions, but always without losing contact with their initial concreteness. And as words are used with such freedom, they function evocatively to shape and power our experience in new ways.

Being "In Place" and Displaced

I want now to focus on one specific pair of metaphors which speak of place. Paul Tournier has characterized the language of disorientation and reorientation in terms of (1) finding one's place, and (2) leaving one's place for another.[1] The drama of

1. Tournier, *A Place for You.*

disorientation and reorientation is as old in the Bible as the call to Abram and Sarai to leave their place and go to another: "Now Yahweh said to Abram, 'Go from your land and from your kin-group and from your father's house to the land that I will show you'" (Genesis 12:1). It is as pertinent as Jesus calling to the disciples to leave everything and to follow him.

> And passing along by the Sea of Galilee, he saw Simon and Andrew, Simon's brother, casting a net in the sea, for they were fishers. And Jesus said to them, "Follow me and I will make you become fishers of people." And immediately they left their nets and followed him. And going on a bit farther, he saw James the son of Zebedee and John his brother, who were in their boat mending the nets. And immediately he called them; and they left their father, Zebedee, in the boat with the hired servants and followed him. (Mark 1:16–20)

I do not suggest that these particular metaphors and images are any more important than others might be. But I pursue them as suggestive of the imaginative work of linkage that must be done in the praying of the Psalms.

The image of place in the Psalms suggests that in different places one prays different prayers. There are specific kinds of language appropriate to the situation in which one finds one's self. Speech about place is speech that enables both parties, speaker and God, to be clear about the nature of the interaction. The well-known Shaker song has it,

> 'Tis a gift to be simple,
>> 'tis a gift to be free.
> 'Tis a gift to come down
>> where you ought to be.

We shall explore two images of place, one which finds Israel finally where it ought to be, the other which finds Israel in the utterly wrong place.

The "Pit" as the Wrong Place

The speech of the wrong place is, of course, found in the prayers of disorientation. In the complaints, there is a great deal of talk about the pit. First, we know that the pit has concrete reality as a place in which to put people to render them null and void. In the pit, people are effectively removed from life. Historically, this is the device used for Joseph by his brothers (Genesis 37:22, 28) and for the prophet Jeremiah by his enemies (Jeremiah 38:6–9). The pit is used against enemies. It means to deny to a person all the resources necessary for life. Those in the pit experience a "social death" (as social scientists call it) because they are cut off from family and community and can exercise no control over their own lives. It is therefore not difficult to see how the specific reference became an embracive symbol for death. The pit reduces one to powerlessness.

It is of course difficult in the Psalms, as in any powerful poetry, to know when a word is being used descriptively and when it is being used metaphorically. But that is the power of this language. It always can have both tendencies. And it is probable that even the speaker was not always clear which way the word should be taken. That is why we may return again and again to these words. Each time we bring something different. And each time we find the Psalms' words shaped and nuanced in fresh ways.

Thus pit refers to the experience of being rendered powerless. In Psalm 28:1, to "be like those who go to the pit [Hebrew *bôr*]," means to be silent, forgotten, dead. This is clearly a cry of disorientation, for the speaker fears losing the old relation with Yahweh, knowing then that everything is lost. In Psalm 88, the language is fuller. The speaker is characterized as having no strength and as being forsaken (vv. 4–5), among the dead, slain, not remembered, cut off. The image evokes a torrent of words. The image is repeated in v. 6, expressed as dark and deep; and in v. 7, there is reference to the flood waters of chaos that will overwhelm. Thus the image tends to slide easily over into another one. If we were to use psychological language in the consideration of this Psalm, perhaps we would regard this as "severe depression." But the imagery of the Psalm cuts underneath psychology to talk about the multi-faceted experience involved. The poets are powerful in being able to bring such a struggle to visibility and concreteness. Notice that even though there is great detail, one cannot determine from the Psalm what the actual problem is —whether sickness, abandonment, guilt, imprisonment. The poet has an amazing capacity to say much and yet leave everything open. Thus the Psalm provides a marvelous receptacle which we are free to fill with our particular experience.

A different Hebrew word (*šaḥat*), but with the same effect, is used in Psalm 30:9, which asserts that the pit is a place cut off from God so that God may neither help nor be praised there:

> What profit is there in my death,
>> if I descend into the pit [*šaḥat*]?
> Will the dust praise you?
>> Will it proclaim your faithfulness?

In Psalm 35:7–8, there is a statement of attack against enemies who prepared the pit, so that dislocation may bring about a turning to God not only for vindication but for vengeance.

The cry for vengeance is a powerful part of disorientation. Such a cry blames those who have disrupted and demolished the old equilibrium. Thus in addition to the yearning to be saved from the pit, there is the counter-theme of wishing others would be sent there. There is nothing pious or "Christian" about this prayer. But (as psychotherapists know), our deep disorientation is not a time when we are able to be genuinely humane toward others because we are singularly attentive to the lack of humanness in our own life.

Thus there is the wish that the ones who have created the pit should be in it (9:15; compare 94:13). In addition to the concrete word for pit, there is use of the word Sheol. This word has been mistakenly translated "hell." It does not refer to anything like that, for classical Israelite thought did not envision a place of ultimate punishment. Rather, the term refers simply to a place of undifferentiated, powerless, gray existence where one is removed from joy, and discourse with God. There is the wish that the troublemakers should go there:

> Let death come upon them;
>> let them descend alive into Sheol;
> for evil is in their homes and in their hearts.
> (Psalm 55:15; see also 31:17; 141:7)

Most remarkably, the dark, discouraging, deathly image of pit (cistern, ruin, Sheol) is used not only to describe a hopeless situation and to offer a counter-wish of the same for one's enemies. The image suggests also that there is real movement in its use. Those who stay with the image are able to speak not only in prospect of the pit or in the midst of trouble, but also after the trouble, in a mood of joy. The image occurs not only in songs of disorientation but in psalms of thanksgiving which sing of reorientation:

> O Yahweh, you have brought my life up from *Sheol,*
> > restored me to life from among those gone
> > > down to the *pit* [*bôr*]. (Psalm 30:3)

> He drew me up from the desolate *pit* [*bôr*],
> > out of the *miry bog.* (Psalm 40:2)

> For thou dost not give me up to *Sheol,*
> > or let thy godly one see the *pit* [*šaḥat*].
> > (Psalm 16:10)

> You have delivered my soul from the depths of *Sheol.*
> (Psalm 86:13)

We may note one other use which is of interest. The same motif is used in the song of thanksgiving in Jonah 2:

> out of the belly of *Sheol* I cried,
> > and you heard my voice. (v. 2)
> I went down to the land
> > whose bars closed upon me forever;
> yet you brought up my life from the pit [*bôr*],
> > O Yahweh, my God. (v. 6)

In its present context, the reference purports to refer to the experience in the fish, but clearly the psalm itself has an independent existence. Thus the reference to Sheol in v. 2 and pit in v. 6 can be filled with various content, depending on the circumstance of the speaker.

It is clear that the metaphor reports movement, first the cry of anguish about the pit, second the cry of vengeance, and third the voice of thanksgiving. The image permits the speaker to stay with the experience and see it through. The motif of pit enables the speaker to present every posture of life to God. Clearly the metaphor of pit in itself is of no interest to the Psalms, but it is a way of bringing life to God to have it dealt with.

So we have considered the concrete and metaphorical uses. Now, third, it remains that the contemporary user of the Psalms should take the image of pit and locate those experiences and dimensions of one's own life which are "the pits." This may include powerlessness, being abandoned, forgotten, lonely, helpless, cheated. It may be something as concrete as remembering being "stood in the corner" at school. Or it may be as powerful as a black person being made to "stay in his place," or a woman oppressed all this time by finding her only place to be the kitchen.

Such occurrences in our lives can, with the help of the Psalms, be given concrete expression, and we can begin the process of moving past them—perhaps even to a song of celebration and thanksgiving. These Psalms attest to us that the life of faith does not protect us from the pit. Rather, the power of God brings us out of the pit to new life which is not the same as pre-pit existence. When one is in the pit, one cannot believe or imagine that good can come again. For that reason, the Psalmist finally focuses not on the pit but on the One who rules there and everywhere. It is the reality of God which makes clear that the pit is not the place "where you ought to be."

Under Safe Wings

Let us consider, in an abrupt transition, a second figure for place which is in every way contrasted with the first. A favorite image of Israel for a safe place with God is to speak of being safe under the protective wings of God. Whereas pit speaks of danger and threat, wings speak of safety, tenderness, and nurture. There is no doubt that the image is consciously derived from the concrete observation of how little birds are safe under the protective wing of the mother hen:

> As an eagle stirs up its nest,
>> and hovers over its young;
> as it spreads its *wings,* takes them up,
>> and bears them aloft on its pinions,
> Yahweh alone guided him . . .
>> (Deuteronomy 32:11–12a; see Matthew 23:37;
>> Luke 13:34)

But obviously the concrete reference becomes a metaphor which is much used in the songs of complaint. It is a figure that yearns for safety, well-being, communion with God, or—in our language—a new orientation:

> Keep me as the apple of your eye;
>> hide me in the shadow of your *wings.* (Psalm 17:8)

> Be merciful to me, O God . . .
>> for in you my soul takes *refuge,*
> in the shadow of your *wings*
>> I will take *refuge.* (Psalm 57:1)

Now it may occur to some that this image is an image of dependency in which one engages in a religious cop-out from the realities of life. That is a possible reading. But the image does not need to be understood as escapism. It may rather be discerned as evangelical realism, acknowledging that the resources for life are not found in "us" but will have to come from another source outside of self. It is the recognition of the disoriented person that a new orientation must come as a gift. Thus the metaphor embodies an openness to a new purpose, a submission to the will of another, a complete reliance upon the protective concern of another. The two images, protective wing and refuge (which is of the genre of fortress and thus a war image) occur together in the supplication of Psalm 61:2a–4:

> Lead me
>> to the *rock* that is higher than I;
> for you are my *refuge,*
>> a *strong tower* against the enemy.
> Let me dwell in your *tent* for ever!
>> O to be safe under the *shelter of your wings*!

Notice here the cluster of images to which are added *tent, rock,* and *tower,* all used together to contrast with the current situation of need.

As with pit, so these images are not confined to situations of distress. And therefore they occur not only in the complaints and supplications, but also in speeches of confidence and trust, rather as conclusions drawn from long experience. These are the voices of the reoriented:

> The children of men take refuge in the *shadow of your wings*. (Psalm 36:7)

> You would confound the plans of the poor,
>   but Yahweh is his *refuge*. (Psalm 14:6; cf. 46:1)

These statements have the effect of vetoing the claim of the pit, of denying the pit the capacity to terrorize completely. They assert not that God will be or has promised to be a refuge, but that God is refuge right in the present circumstance. And therefore the words serve to redefine radically the place of the pray-er. He is verbally transported from the pit to the wing, from the place of powerlessness to utter safety, i.e., from death to life. And this change happens in the bold, free play of evocative language.

Our two positive images occur together in a remarkable psalm of trust:

> He who dwells in the *shelter* of the Most High,
>   who abides in the shadow of the Almighty,
> will say to Yahweh, my *refuge* and my *fortress,*
>   my God in whom I trust . . .
> Because you have made Yahweh your *refuge* . . .
>   no evil shall befall you . . . (Psalm 91:1–2, 9)

The capacity to speak the Psalms in the full freedom of imagination is already the embrace of a new orientation, an entry into the kingdom of God. It is of course possible that the words outdistance the realities. They could be spoken when an observer might conclude that the person is still in fact in the pit. But we live in pursuit of our imagination. Thus the use of the Psalm of trust while still in the pit is an act of profound hope which permits new life. Expressing one's trust in God's sheltering wings is a bold assertion that the power of the pit has been broken. Imaginative speech may outdistance actual circumstance. But it is a first gesturing of transformed circumstance.

This Psalm (91) is a remarkable convergence of motifs. In addition to our two images, it offers a variety of war images (vv. 4–8) which can usefully be explored and exploited. It offers animal imagery in v. 13 and speaks in v. 11 that marvelous offer, "He will give his angels charge of you." It concludes in vv. 14–16 with one of those rare responses of God which utterly transform. The self-assertion of God is a response to the boldness of submission:

- I will deliver
- I will protect
- I will answer
- I will be with
- I will rescue
- I will honor
- I will satisfy
- I will show

Finally concerning this metaphor, we should mention its surprising use in Ruth 2:12, where it is used in a narrative, when Boaz says to Ruth in the field:

> May Yahweh reward you for your actions, and may you have a full reward from Yahweh, the God of Israel, under whose *wings* you have come for *refuge*.

Here, in communication on a human plane, the same image transforms a social situation.

In the Move from Pit to Wing

Our lives always move between the pit and the wing, between the shattering of disorientation and the gift of life. That is what our baptism is about—to die and to rise with him to newness of life (Romans 6:1–11).

It remains for those who use this metaphor, like every other, to identify those events and experiences in which hovering wings have cared, in which we have been made utterly safe and so free that life has begun again. Every man, woman, and child of us has been within and shall again face the pit, and this must be brought to speech. Every one of us has the wings assured to us (see Deuteronomy 33:27), and that also must be spoken about.

It is clear that the Psalms, when we freely engage ourselves with them, are indeed subversive literature. They break things loose. They disrupt and question. They open up new possibilities. They create new relationships. Most of all, they give us new eyes to see and new tongues to speak. And therefore, we need not enter the Presence of the Holy One mute and immobilized. We go there to practice our vocation of receiving the new future God is speaking to us. To risk such prayer is to repent of the old orientation to which we no longer belong. It is to refuse the pit which must first be fully experienced for the sake of the wings which may be boldly anticipated.

4

Christians in
"Jewish Territory"

❈ THE PSALMS ARE A CENTERPIECE OF CHRIS-
tian liturgy, piety, and spirituality. They have been so from the
beginning of the Christian movement for good reason. They
have been found poignant in expression, able to empower
believing imagination in remarkable ways. This is evident
in the rich use made of the Psalms through the New Testament, most especially in the passion of Jesus. But the use of
the Psalms by Christians is not without awkwardness, for the
Psalms are relentlessly Jewish in their mode of expression and
in their faith claims. And with our best intent for generosity
and good faith, the different nuances of Jewish and Christian
faith are not to be overlooked or easily accommodated.

What Christians appropriate from the Psalms for worship and piety surely arose in a variety of Jewish settings, or,
before Judaism, in the environment of ancient Israel. We do
not know a great deal about such initial venues for the Psalms,
but we do know some things. There is no doubt that the Jerusalem temple in the monarchal period was a generator of
Psalms. In the Second Temple period, moreover, the guilds
of "temple singers," attested in 1 and 2 Chronicles, produced
more Psalms. And outside of Jerusalem, other prominent sanc-
tuaries (such as Gilgal, Bethel, and Shiloh) produced Psalms.
It is for that reason that the Book of Psalms is a "collection

of collections." The end product—altogether Jewish—is an ecumenical achievement that drew together a rich variety of local traditions.

Christian Modes of Avoidance

Two characteristic ways of handling this issue in the Psalms are easily identifiable. The first way is to be highly selective and make use of those Psalms that are most congenial to us and that contain the least objectionable "Jewishness." We may do this by completely avoiding some Psalms, for example, Psalm 109, because it is too full of rancor and venom, or Psalm 137, which too harshly expresses its passion for brutal retaliation. These, it would seem at first glance, have no acceptable place in "conventional Christian faith." Or we may make our selection more delicately and only screen out certain verses. Thus for example, in Psalm 145, a marvelous statement of trust, v. 20b comes as a shattering negative at the end and is usually left off. Or Psalm 95:1–7a is a much used call to worship. But vv. 7b–11 are judged excessively concrete and negative—even though the writer of Hebrews found these verses pertinent in an appeal for Christian fidelity (Hebrews 3:7–11 and 4:3–11). We may make our selections on grounds other than those used by the New Testament.

But note, we have spoken about "conventional Christian faith." There is, to be sure, a broad body of the Psalms that is unobjectionable in this regard. They move in a much broader, more irenic pattern of rhetoric. They speak in a way that lends itself to any serious religious commitment without being excessively concrete. Sensitivity to "Jewish awkwardness" has led much Christian practice to stay on this "safe" ground. But obviously that is to avoid and not confront the question we seek to face here.

The other characteristic way (not unrelated to the first) is to claim that Christianity, especially the New Testament, evolved from and is superior to the Old Testament Jewishness and thus supersedes it and can disregard "objectionable parts." On the one hand, this may lead us to imagine Christians have "outgrown" the offensive Jewishness of the Psalms and so legitimate the criteria for selectivity noted above. On the other hand, Jewish motifs are retained but "spiritualized." That is, they are taken to refer to matters other than the concrete referent. This may permit "christological" interpretation. Especially is this true of reference to "Jerusalem" (compare Psalms 84:7; 122:6; 147:2), which may be taken to refer to Jesus, to a heavenly Jerusalem, only less concretely to any place of worship or meaning.

Again, a long-standing practice (going back to very early Christian interpretation) is to treat the Psalms as claims about Jesus Christ. In the tradition of Augustine, for example, there is a tendency to find hints about the life, ministry, death, and resurrection of Jesus at many points in the Psalms.

It is not easy to know how to assess such a practice. On the one hand, it may seem to make the Psalms more readily available for Christian use. On the other hand, I suggest such "spiritualizing" tends to tone the Psalms down and avoid the abrasive and offensive elements. On balance, I believe it more helpful to avoid such a practice. We will be helped to a more genuine piety and an authentic faith if we engage the Psalms as poetry about our common, particular humanness. Nothing should be done that detracts from that reality. Facing such a

"Christian" alternative, we should be more attentive to the rawness of Jewish faith out of which the Psalms speak.

But there is another alternative. It is in the prayers of Jesus that we may link Jewish ways of praying and christological interpretation. For the prayers of Jesus are surely prayers of a Jew. He prayed as a Jew. And the entire tradition of Christian prayer and Christian use of the Psalms must be seen in this light. This gives us warrant for christological interpretation, but the centrality of Jesus can never be far separated from the Jewish character of the material.

We are now, especially because of the Holocaust, at a new place in Jewish-Christian conversations. Old presuppositions and behaviors will no longer do. We are at a new place where we must take each other with a new kind of seriousness, albeit with a new kind of awkwardness. It is clear that either selectivity or spiritualizing in fact simply avoids the resilient Jewishness of the Psalms. Moreover, our new situation makes clear that something urgent is at stake for us Christians in this question. It is clear that embrace of Jewishness in the Psalter must be faced not for the sake of the Jews, not out of respect because we are "persons of good will," not out of a notion of brotherhood. Rather, the Jewishness of the Psalms must be faced because our spirituality is diminished and trivialized if we neglect the Jewishness that belongs to our own tradition and practice of faith. It is for our sake and not the sake of the Jews that we are pressed to make this dimension of the Psalms our own. This is an exceedingly difficult and complex issue, not to be resolved here. Perhaps three aspects of the problem can provide a beginning both for our common prayer and for our educational tasks.

Praying for Jews

The Jewishness of the Psalms invites us to pray for the Jews. This is not meant to be a condescension, as though our prayers matter more than theirs. Nor does it mean praying for conversion of the Jews—the commonness of our faith precludes any such issue. Rather, it means to bring to utterance the deepest longings, echoes, and yearnings of the Jews, for Jews are a paradigm of the deepest longings and yearnings of all of humanity. And we dare say that in them we may hear even the profound sighs of the Almighty who must also practice something very Jewish in "his" day-to-day sojourn.

And for every brand of Jewishness (Zionist or not), these aches and yearnings have to do with Jerusalem. (See Luke 13:34–35; 19:41–44, where Jesus aches and groans over Jerusalem.) In the matrix of the Holocaust and the modern state of Israel, both present yearnings and future hopes as well as remembered anguishes are linked to Jerusalem.

To pray for Jews is to recognize how pervasive is zeal for Zion in the Psalms. Externally, this may be so because the completed Psalter was undoubtedly shaped by priestly and/or political interests for whom Jerusalem is the center of the universe. Thus the Jerusalem interest has a tinge of ideology in the Psalms. It is true that Jerusalem has emerged as a gathering and focusing symbol for all of Israel's life. It embodies the memory of great political power under David and Solomon. It articulates the assurance of God's presence near his creation and among his folk (Isaiah 4:2–6). It holds the promise of a world of justice and peace:

> In days to come the mountain of Yahweh's house
>> shall be established as the highest of the mountains
>> and shall be raised above the hills.
> All the countries shall stream to it.
>> Many peoples shall come and say,
> "Come, let us go up to Yahweh's mountain
>> to the house of the God of Jacob;
> that he may teach us his ways
>> and that we may walk in his paths." (Isaiah 2:2–4)

As Christians sing with another referent, so Jews may and must sing of Jerusalem.

"The hopes and fears of all the years are met in thee tonight." That carol which sings "tonight" is not very different from the formula from the night of the Passover, "next year in Jerusalem"—the Jewish rendition of the biblical dream of justice, freedom, and well-being. Thus after the entry into the Psalter by way of the Torah in Psalter 1, the Psalter moves to Zion in 2:6 and concludes at Zion in 149:2. With Jews, we can pray for the peace of Jerusalem (Psalm 122:6). With Jews, we may set Jerusalem above our highest joy (Psalm 137:6). With Zion, we are summoned to praise the Lord (Psalm 147:12). Indeed, Psalm 128:5 suggests that Jerusalem is always on the tip of the tongue, even when the agenda is something else (see Psalms 2:6; 122:6; 147:12; 149:2).

To be sure, we may know at the same time that in the end time, true worship is not "placed," but is in "spirit and in truth" (John 4:20–24). But in the meantime. . . . So there is a tension. We cannot leave Jerusalem as the flat, one-dimensional city of cynical Solomon. But also, we cannot run away from Jerusalem, for it embodies the meanings and the hopes, the fears and yearnings of our faith tradition. And we know that it also embodies the best yearnings of most of humanity. The reality of Jerusalem keeps alive among us the conviction that the world is not closed and fixed. Something more is promised. And for that we wait. Praying for Jews means the practice of a solidarity in concrete hope that is old and deep in our faith.

Praying with Jews

When we have prayed for Jews, by turning to Jewish shapes of reality, then in our use of the Psalms, we may perchance pray with the Jews. Our prayer life is always sorely tempted to individualism or at least to parochialism. We are urged by God's spirit to pray along-side and so to be genuinely ecumenical.

As we use the Psalms, it is appropriate to ask which Jews have used these same Psalms with passion and at risk. And a parade of victims comes to our imagination. Or, with more immediacy, which Jews now pray these Psalms, from the frightened victims of anti-Semitism to the fated soldiers in the Israeli army, to the Jews in our own culture who are forever displaced and always at the brink of rejection and despisement. To pray with Jews is to be aware of the solidarity with the chosen of God whom the world rejects. To be sure, the Jews are an enigma, and we cannot ever identify that people by any simple category. But they stand as an odd testimony that God stands by and with and for those whom the world rejects.

To pray with introduces a fresh agenda into our Christian spirituality:

1. It tilts us toward a very specific history as our history. Thus, for example, see Psalms 78, 105, 106, 136, which provide a history of betrayal and disobedience, of surprise and deliverance. That history that becomes ours in prayer is a minority history, a history of victims and marginal people. But we need not romanticize. This history is also a memory of grasping and not trusting and thereby bringing trouble. That history may be a critique of our usual histories on which we count too heavily, a history of a triumphal church or an imperial nation or an intolerant culture. Praying with may lead us to another, converted identity.

2. Jews cannot pray very long without meditating on the Torah (Psalms 1; 19; 119). The Torah at the center of spirituality may deliver us from excessive romanticism or mysticism or subjectivity. Jewish preoccupation with the Torah is hard-nosed realism about the given norms of our life, about the ethical context of our faith, about the public character of true religion. The Torah at the center reminds us that the primal mode of faithfulness and knowing God is obedience. These Jewish prayers are affirming and joyous, celebrative of the realization that the Torah is not only command but assurance, not only a rule but a bulwark. Reality is structured in ways that will not be defeated. And power is given to share in this God-ordained structuring of reality. Life has a moral coherence on which we can rely. That moral coherence (experienced as obedience) makes a difference to the keeping of God's promises.

3. To pray with Jews means to live with them in the hope and danger of real judgment. There is no doubt in the

Psalter that God takes folks seriously. On the one hand, God takes folks seriously and lets us have what we choose (Psalms 1:4–6; 2:7; 50:16–18; 145:20). But on the other hand, the arena for spirituality is this: Jews know that this God who honors our ways is the same God who overrides our ways:

> Yahweh is merciful and gracious,
>> slow to anger and abounding in loyalty.
> He will not always accuse,
>> nor will he hold on to his anger forever.
> He does not deal with us according to our sins,
>> nor repay us according to our transgressions . . . .
> For he knows how we were made;
>> he remembers that we are dust.
> (Psalm 103:8–10, 14; see also 19:12–13; 130:3–5)

This tension lies at the heart of spirituality in the Psalms. The tension is that God gives us permission to choose our futures and, at the same time, God chooses a future for us that is gracious beyond our choosing. This tension must be lived with and not resolved. It must not be reduced to a scholastic problem of freedom and predestination. In each psalm, each moment must be taken for itself and not yielded easily to some alternative claim or to some overarching scheme. The Jewish awkwardness with which we must contend concerns a special history as the elect ones, a special claim in the Torah which assumes and compels, and a special awe before the reality of God's judgment and mercy.

To pray with Jews means to stay as long as these poems do at the raw edge with a live God who will not let us settle easily or for too long. There is a precariousness in this life of faith. Jews have known that for a very long time. Such prayer is risky because we have to do here with a God who is himself precarious and at risk. And the gift of the Jews in this literature is that we may be engaged with this very same God.

Praying as Jews

If we could genuinely pray for Jews and pray with Jews, then perhaps we can risk this presumption. (It is of course an enormously presumptuous thing for a Gentile to suggest, but we must not lose nerve in receiving the gift of these texts.) In the providence of God, we might be permitted (and required) to pray as Jews. I state the point with uneasiness. The uneasiness is of two kinds. First, it is impossible to identify Jewishness, and so it is too bold to say what it is to be "as Jews." Second, becoming a Jew takes many centuries and many generations. And I am under no romantic illusions about quick transformations. Few of us have lamented in Babylon or been close enough to the ovens when they have been heated. But given those admissions and misgivings, let us hint at five dimensions of Jewishness which mark the Psalms, dimensions that might matter to our spirituality.

I make no claim that these marks are essentially "Jewish." But I speak of them this way on two grounds. First, they seem to me to be facets of the Psalms which are most troublesome to us, which Christians most prefer to screen out as awkward and offensive. Second, even if they are not definitively Jewish, they at least stand in contrast to the dominant "Greek" reasonableness and idealism which have shaped our spirituality. What I have called "Jewish" at least contrasts with the cool, detached serenity (not to say apathy) of which we are inheritors (and too often practitioners).

1. *The Psalms are awkward in their concreteness.* They do not engage in sweeping generalizations to which we are observers. The imagery and speech is pointed and specific. This is true of the historical references to Zion, to king, to enemies. Psalmic rhetoric is concrete about commandments and punishments, about angers, loves, and hopes. Such a way of prayer may be a trouble when we want to pray "in general" without focusing anywhere. The "cultural despisers" of biblical faith consistently want a generalized religious consciousness and are offended by God become concrete. In Israel, this scandal is in God's way with the "nobodies":

> Yahweh upholds all who are falling,
> and raises up all who are bowed down. (Psalm 145:14)

In the New Testament, the same scandal is in Jesus of Nazareth:

> Go and tell John what you have seen and heard:
> the blind receive their sight, the lame walk, those
> with skin diseases are cleansed, the deaf hear, the
> dead are raised, the poor have good news delivered
> to them. And how honorable is the one who takes
> no offense at me. (Luke 7:22–23)

The Psalms are "embodied" prayers.

2. *There is no or little slippage between what is thought/felt and what is said.* The Psalms are immediate. There is no mediation to "clean up," censor, or filter what is going on. This directness reflects a readiness to risk in an uncalculating way with this one "from whom no secret can be hid." The Psalms dare to affirm that, as there are no secrets hid from God, so there likely is less self-deception at work in these prayers. These

prayers are marked by candor and robustness with the God who "searches the heart" (Jeremiah 17:10; Proverbs 20:27). These are the prayers of the liberated, who in their freedom are able to speak in an artistic way without ornamentation. Liberated prayer of this kind is filled with passion, i.e., with the conviction that in these words, something is at issue that can be resolved in more than one way. And which of the ways of resolution depends on how the prayer engages the person of God.

There are not many evidences in the Psalms of depression, either psychological or spiritual. There are active passions such as rage, anger, and hatred, but this is contrasted with the immobility of depression. These Psalms in their candor are on the one hand sung because the singers have been liberated. On the other hand, these very songs are an act of emancipation. The songs both reflect and accomplish liberation. (It is no wonder that the therapeutic tradition of emancipation grows from this resilient and bold Jewish vision.) In the language of R. D. Laing, there is no split here between "experience" and "behavior."[1] What Israel experiences in the struggle of faith is what it speaks in its behavior of the Psalms. In this identity of thought/feeling and speech, the Psalms overcome the calculating and careful distance that characterizes very much "polite" piety. Prayer stays very close to the realities of life in these poems.

3. *The robustness and candor of the Psalms are especially evident in the articulation of hatred and anger.* There is no thought here that Israel must be on good behavior in the presence of God. Everything at work in life is readily brought to

1. Laing, *The Politics of Experience,* especially chapter 1.

expression. This prayer is an expression of "no more Mr. Nice Guy." Perhaps this freedom is birthed in the Exodus event, in which Israel knows early that Pharaoh first must be identified as the enemy and then must be verbally assaulted. There is no courteous yearning for reconciliation here. Life is known to be conflicted. And therefore, the practice of conflicted and conflicting speech is necessary. Israel at prayer is ready to carry on linguistic assault against its enemies, one of whom is sometimes God. (Thus, it is not unimportant that Job, that most honest of pray-ers in Israel, is named "enemy." That is, the word Job means "enemy." Israel at prayer is prepared to speak as enemy.) Israel does not envision a false community in which unequal partners love each other in their unjust and unequal positions.

Well before the New Testament, the Psalmists endorsed the notion, "be angry but do not sin" (Ephesians 4:26; see Psalm 4:4). Anger is here in abundance. And anger is topped by hatred. The true believer hates powerfully and finds a community with Yahweh (the God of Israel) who also hates:

> Do I not hate those who hate you, O Yahweh?
>> And do I not loathe them that rise up against you?
> I hate them with perfect hatred;
>> I count them my enemies. (Psalm 139:21–22)

Indeed, the speaker, like Yahweh, is never passive or apathetic. Of course it might be objected that the speaker too readily identifies his own hatred with that of God. Perhaps so. But in the moment of hatred, that is what happens to all of us. This anger is not only spiritually liberated. It is psychologically honest. It asserts what each of us in our moment of insane hatred tends to do. In that moment, we are incapable of maintaining critical distance from our own sensitivities.

God as well is one who is capable of hatred for evildoers (Psalms 5:5; 31:16). Our objection to the Psalms' expression of hatred reflects our notion that God is incapable of such a posture. But that is how it is with the God of the Psalms. Such a conviction about God permits this practice of piety.

And the rage goes even deeper. The rage born of anger and hatred can be turned against God. In a no-holds-barred extremity, Job articulates venom even against God:

> Though I am innocent, my own mouth would condemn me;
> > though I am blameless, he would prove me perverse . . .
> It is all one;
> > therefore I say, he destroys both the blameless and the
> > wicked. (Job 9:20, 22)

There is something peculiarly Jewish about such a posture that completely re-identifies both God and the speaker. Here is no "unmoved mover," no object to be adored, no "Ground of Being." Here is the Ultimate Partner who must enter the fray and be at issue along with the speaker. It should be clear that the Jewish interaction between the two, God and prayer, is contrasted with our conventional piety. And we learn so slowly that such candid piety speaks to what is really at stake. Risky as it is, this piety makes a genuine, healing difference in life. And as such, it serves as an important model for human interaction as well.

4. *But Israel is not able only to rage with abandon. Israel has equal passion for hope.* Elie Wiesel, that most remarkable storyteller from the Holocaust, has said that what makes a

Jew a Jew is this inability to quit hoping. Jewishness consists in "going on," in persisting, in hoping. In writing of his encounter with Saul Lieberman, Wiesel writes of tenacity as it is related to the reality of God:

> What I learned from him is what, of all my knowledge, I value most. He made me aware that to be a Jew is to place the greatest store in knowledge and loyalty, that it is because he recognizes divine justice that he speaks out against human injustice. That it is because a Jew remains attached to his God that he is permitted to question Him. It is because the prophets loved the people of Israel that they admonished them and reprimanded their kings. Everything depends on where you stand, my master used to say. With God anything can be said. Without God nothing is heard. Without God what is said is not said.[2]

Whatever the psychological elements of hope are, the structure of hope is the conviction of a new world. A new gift from God is at work on our behalf. And this new gift from God is at work, critiquing, dismantling, and transforming the present age which is so characterized by injustice and enmity. It is characteristically Jewish to hope for newness from God, from this specific God who is a giver of newness. Here is no fascination with "being." Even "nature" is understood as creation, called by God to bring forth newness:

> You visit the earth and water it;
> > you greatly enrich it.
> The river of God is full of water;
> > you provide the people with grain,

2. Wiesel, *Memoirs*, 380.

for you have prepared it.
(Psalm 65:9; see 145:13b–16)

It will not do (as Claus Westermann,[3] Samuel Terrien,[4] and
Rolf Knierim[5] have shown) to focus on historical events to
the neglect of the structure and character of "nature." But
"nature" as well (better "creation"), is not fixed and settled. It
also lives under hope and will be transformed for the new age.
Thus Israel hopes for the structures of creation as well as for
the specificity of human communities.

Following Westermann, Erhard Gerstenberger has seen
that even the complaint psalms are acts of hope.[6] They articulate the deepest hurt, anger, and rage of Israel. But they
are not statements of resignation which accept the bad situation. Rather, they are insistences upon and expectations from
God, who can and will, may and must, keep promises. Many
examples could be cited. With two different words, Psalm 71
presents this deep hope:

For you, O Lord, art my hope,
    my trust, O Yahweh, from my youth. . . .
But I will hope continually,
    and I will praise you yet more and more. (vv. 5, 14)

3. Westermann has most fully articulated this viewpoint in *What Does
the Old Testament Say about God?,* especially chapter 3. His earlier succinct
statement is "Creation and History in the Old Testament."

4. Terrien, *The Elusive Presence.*

5. Knierim, "Cosmos and History."

6. See Gerstenberger's work, "Der klagende Mensch." For a
contemporary explication of this insight, see Gerstenberger and Wolfgang
Schrage, *Suffering,* 130–35.

Notice the hope is rooted in God, not in the situation. And hope is affirmed precisely in the face of mocking enemies (vv. 10–13).

5. *The practice of concreteness and candor, of anger and hope, is carried out with exceeding passion in the Psalms.* They prepare us for the most striking and problematic element of Jewish prayer, the readiness to seek vengeance. We will delay for now any extended discussion of the topic and take it up separately in the next chapter. For now we must do two things. First, we must recognize that vengeance is both central and problematic in the Psalms. Second, we must recognize that such a yearning for revenge occurs not in a vacuum, but precisely in the context of the qualities we have already presented as characteristically Jewish. The seeking of revenge should be expected from a people who hate and hope with such passion. A religion which practices candor and a piety which is specific will predictably give vent to the yearning for revenge.

As "Jews of Tomorrow"

Notice that these five elements which concern praying as Jews provide a critique of much Christian spirituality. Our suggestion is not that we simply observe these factors as interesting items in the Psalms. Rather, the Psalms are an invitation to transform our piety and liturgy in ways that will make both piety and liturgy somewhat risky and certainly abrasive. Lewis Mumford has written of the relentless Jewish resistance to every assimilation.[7] Jewishness, wherever it occurs, is an awkwardness to those who want to create a "universal cul-

7. Mumford, *The Myth of the Machine*, 232–33.

ture," or a "preachable kingdom." The practice of Jewish piety maintains its odd angularity. And that angularity has dangerous public implications. Obviously a people so passionate in prayer will not willingly practice silent subservience in public life. A community so laden with visions of Torah will not be silent in the streets about injustice. Prayers with and for and as the people of Jerusalem will not long acquiesce in public violation of these visions.

Finally, a word in anticipation of response to these comments. Surely it will occur to some that such an insistence on Jewishness, and especially Jerusalem, is not very evenhanded toward the current political issues surrounding Israel and Jerusalem. My comments have important political implications, but not of that kind.

The theological claims I have made here for Jewishness cut in various ways concerning historical responsibility and political reality. There is a closed kind of Jewishness that can become politically totalitarian. Such a Jewishness is no doubt at work in the modern world, and no doubt one can find some warrant in the Psalms. But there is another kind of Jewishness in the Psalter. And it is to that alternative Jewishness that attention must be drawn. The tension we face in the Psalms (and everywhere in the Old Testament) is the tension between largeness of vision and passion for particularity. Thus far, we have focused on the passion for particularity because I judge that to be the stumbling block for many Christians who face the Psalms.

But largeness of vision is not antithetical to such a passion for particularity. It grows out of it. The elect people bear witness to an all-inclusive providence. So the counter-theme to Jewish particularity is a vision of all peoples who may also be citizens of Jerusalem (cf. Isaiah 2:2–4, Revelation 21:1–4) or who may be reckoned as distinct from Israel but nonetheless part of the fulfillment of God's promise (Isaiah 19:23–25).

1. The Psalms have a passion for the righteous, for the practitioners of God's vision for justice and peace (Psalms 1:5–6; 7:9; 11:7; 34:15; 92:12). And the Psalms are reluctant to equate this commitment with any narrow community. In its largeness of vision, Israel knows there are "Torah keepers" in various communities, some of which bear other names (Isaiah 56:6–8).

2. The Psalms have a passion for the poor and needy (Psalms 69:33; 109:31; 140:12), for those broken of spirit and heart (Psalms 34:18; 51:17). God's compassion is not toward an ethnic community nor those with a pedigree, but toward those in special need.

These elements also belong to the Jewishness of the Psalter. Thus as one envisions the drama of Jerusalem and as those who yearn to be "next year in freedom," the pilgrimage to Jerusalem is a strange procession. That procession toward newness includes the Jews who bear a public identity, but it also includes refugees who are remote from the name "Jew." The Jewishness to which the Psalter calls us is not that of "yesterday's Jews" who rest on the faith of their parents (cf. Matthew 3:9), but on the "Jews of tomorrow" who dare to believe God's concrete promises with passion.

There is a strange restlessness and shattering that belongs to Jewishness. When we learn to pray these prayers faithfully, we shall all be scandalized. Thus I propose that, at the end, conventional notions of Jewishness are also placed in question. But that is only at the end, after we have learned the passion and the patience to pray for, with, and as Jews.

5
Vengeance:
Human and Divine

✾ THE MOST TROUBLESOME DIMENSION OF
the Psalms is the agenda of vengeance. It may also be the most
theologically poignant, as we hope to show. The cry for retaliation at one's enemies at least surprises us. We do not expect
to find such a note in "religious" literature. And it may of-
fend us. It does not fit very well in our usual notions of faith,
piety, or spirituality.[1] To some extent, we are prepared for it
by our recognition (in the last chapter) that the Psalms reflect
unabashed concreteness, candor, and passion. The Psalms explore the full gamut of human experience from rage to hope.
Indeed, it would be very strange if such a robust spirituality
lacked such a dimension of vengeance, for we would conclude
that just at the crucial point, robustness had turned to cow-
ardice and propriety. The vitality of the Psalms, if without a
hunger for vengeance, would be a cop-out. But we need have
no fear of that. There is no such failure of nerve, no back-
ing down from this religion on the brink of stridency. Thus
the expression of vengeance is not unnatural, unexpected, or
inappropriate. But that in no way diminishes its problematic
character.

1. See Zenger, *A God of Vengeance?*

The Reality of Vengeance

Let us begin with two acts of realism. First, the yearning for vengeance is there in the Psalms. It is there, without embarrassment, apology, or censor. Whatever we say on the subject must be linked to that undeniable fact. And we are not free to explain it away. If we are genuinely to pray the Psalms, we must try to understand what is happening in such acts of piety. Certainly no expurgated, "selective" version of the Psalms will do. For that is only to push the problem away. Such "selectivity" does not avoid the presence of the motif. Indeed, selective avoidance will cause us to miss the resources that we may find there.

And the counterpart, a second act of realism, is that the yearning for vengeance is here, among us and within us and with power. It is not only there in the Psalms but it is here in the human heart and the human community. When we know ourselves as well as the Psalter knows us, we recognize that we are creatures who wish for vengeance and retaliation. We wish in every way we can to be right and, if not right, at least stronger. Perhaps we do not engage in child abuse or spouse abuse, and we do not urge the death penalty (at least all of us do not). But in lesser ways, we assault verbally or we nurse affronts, waiting for their reversal and satisfaction. It could be that for some few, these passions are absent or that for more of us, they are absent on occasion. But we must not be so romantic as to imagine we have outgrown the eagerness for retaliation. While developmental psychology may discern other more positive yearnings as an ideal, theological realism cannot afford such deception. The real theological problem, I submit, is not that vengeance is there in the Psalms, but that it is here in our midst. And that it is there and here only reflects how attuned the Psalter is to what goes on among us. Thus, we may begin with a recognition of the acute correspondence between what is written there and what is practiced here. The Psalms do "tell it like it is" with us.

So let us begin with such realism about the poetry and about ourselves. The articulation of vengeance leads us to new awarenesses about ourselves. That is, the yearning for vengeance belongs to any serious understanding of human personality. It is important that it is in Psalm 139 that the mystery of human personhood is celebrated:

> O Yahweh, you have searched me
> > and known me.
> You know when I sit down and when I arise;
> > you discern my thoughts from afar.
> (Psalm 139:1–2; see vv. 13–15)

And it is the same Psalm that expresses the capacity for hatred:

> Do I not hate those who hate you, O Yahweh?
> > And do I not loathe those who rise up against you?
> (Psalm 139:21–22)

The capacity for hatred belongs to the mystery of personhood.

1. The Psalms are the rhetorical practice in fullest measure of what is in us. John Calvin describes the Psalms as "An Anatomy of all Parts of the Soul."[2] And so they are. They tell all about us. The Psalms provide space for full linguistic freedom

2. Stated in his Preface to the *Commentary on Psalms*; see Battles, *The Piety of John Calvin,* 27.

in which nothing is censored or precluded. Thus Psalm 109 surely engages in "overkill" in its wishes and prayers against the "wicked." The words pile up like our nuclear stockpiles, without recognizing that nobody needs to be or could possibly be violated in that many ways. But this is not action. It is words, a flight of passion in imagination.

Such imagination, in which the speaker strains to be vivid and venomous and almost exhibitionist, surely performs several functions. (a) It is no doubt cathartic. We need not flinch from the therapeutic value of the Psalms. In our heavily censored society, this is one place left in which it may all be spoken. (b) But it is more than cathartic, more than simply giving expression to what we have felt and known all along. In genuine rage, words do not simply follow feelings. They lead them. It is speech which lets us discover the power, depth, and intensity of the hurt. The Psalms are acts of self-discovery that penetrate the facade of sweet graciousness. (c) The Psalms serve to legitimate and affirm these most intense elements of rage. In such speech, we discover that our words (and feelings) do not destroy the enemy, i.e., they are not as dangerous as we thought. Nor do our words bring judgment from heaven on us. The world (or God) is not as censorious as we feared. Such speech puts rage in perspective. Our feelings brought to speech are not as dangerous or as important as we imagined, as we wished, or as we feared. When they are unspoken, they loom too large, and we are condemned by them. When spoken, our intense thoughts and feelings are brought into a context in which they can be discerned differently. Notice that in Psalm 109, after the long recital of rage through v. 19, the intensity is spent. Then the speaker must return to the reality of heart and fear and helplessness in vv. 22–25. The rage is a prelude to the real agenda of attitudes about one's self.

2. It is important to recognize that these verbal assaults of imagination and hyperbole are verbal. They speak wishes and prayers. But the speaker does not do anything beyond speak. The speech of vengeance is not to be equated with acts of vengeance. This community which respected and greatly valued language encouraged speech, destructive as it might be, in the place of destructive action. So far as we know, even in the most violent cries for vengeance, no action is taken. These Psalms might help us reflect on retaliatory violence in a society which has lost its places and legitimacy for speech. Where there is no valued speech of assault for the powerless, the risks of deathly action are much higher from persons in despair.

3. The speech of vengeance is characteristically offered to God, not directly to the enemy. Thus Psalm 109 begins with an address to God. And in v. 21, the turn from venom to self-reflection happens in, "But you." The final appeal in v. 26 is no longer an urging to action but an imperative that God should act. That is, vengeance is transferred from the heart of the speaker to the heart of God. The Psalm characteristically is structured to show that vengeance is not simply a psychological but a theological matter. It must be referred to God. And when vengeance is entrusted to God, the speaker is relatively free from its power. The speaker, with all the hurt and joy, affirms himself/herself to be God's creature. That recognition of being in God's realm and able to address God gives perspective to the venom.

Thus the movement of the speech is in two parts. First, the vengeance must be fully recognized as present, fully owned as "my" rage, and fully expressed with as much power and intensity as possible. It must be given freedom for full play and visibility. It is analogous to grief. We know grief is best handled by full articulation. And Israel knows that same thing about rage.

But second, this full rage and bitterness is yielded to God's wisdom and providential care. This happens when the speaker finally says, "But thou."[3] The yielding cannot be full and free unless the articulation and owning is first full and freed. The yielding, i.e., submission to God, is an act of faith and confidence. The speaker has no doubt that God will honor and take seriously the need for vengeance and will act upon it. But the doxology of Psalm 109:30–31 makes clear that the final confidence is in God. In this way, the I-Thou relationship is established and maintained. It is based on an awareness of one's self as well as an acknowledgment of God's self.[4] It is not in the rightness of the venom or the legitimacy of the rage. There is no sense of being triumphant, but only of being very sure of God. By the end of such a Psalm, the cry for vengeance is not resolved. The rage is not removed. But it has been dramatically transformed by the double step of owning and yielding.

3. Terrien, in his *The Elusive Presence,* observes the function and power of "Thou" in Psalm 73: "An inquisitive essay has become a prayer. The skeptic, who pondered intellectual answers to difficult questions, suddenly addressed the Deity as 'Thou.' He inserted his doubt into the context of his adoration. . . . Therefore, he no longer pursued his trend of thinking within the confines of his autonomous self but pursued it instead in the presence of the Godhead" (316).

4. See Buber, *I and Thou.*

God's Vengeance and Our Vengeance

But such a prayer still shocks us. And it drives the issue one step further. What about God? What about this God who receives such prayers and at least leaves open the impression that "he"[5] shares the venom and will act on it. We need to begin by recognizing two things about God's self-presentation in the Psalms and in the entire Bible. First, there is no single, coherent picture of God. Nor is there a neat development from a vengeful to a loving God. Rather, there are various sketches and disclosures in different circumstances. Each such disclosure is offered on its own and makes its own claim. And each such sketch must be fully honored on its own without being reduced to a generalized portrait.[6]

Second, every presentation of God is filtered through human imagination. The God presented in any sketch is not untouched by human interest, human need, and human wish. We can easily see that people with passionate hates assign these same hates to God. That is, we find it easy to identify our passions with the passions of God, and collapse the distance between us and the Holy One. But we must recognize that the "nice" presentations of God—as loving, forgiving, merciful—are also filtered through human interest, human need, and human wish.

So we may not easily take some disclosures of God as "more nearly true" simply because we happen to like them. The mystery, sovereignty, and freedom of God require us to

5. Masculine pronouns are placed in quotes to indicate the problem of using masculine language when in fact the language is inclusive. I have appropriated the practice from Gottwald, *The Tribes of Yahweh*, 684–85.

6. See, for example, Brueggemann, *Old Testament Theology*; and Gerstenberger, *Theologies in the Old Testament*.

hold loosely even our preferred sketches of God. And nowhere is this more important than in this question of vengeance. In these poems, we have an "interested," theological statement. But such a statement is not made without authenticity. That is, this is serious speech addressed to a real God, about things genuinely important. And our best theological treatment recognizes that these speeches may articulate our most important concerns to God. And we take these statements seriously only if we regard them as well-intended and deeply felt prayers.

1. The Psalms (and the entire Bible) are clear that vengeance belongs to God (Deuteronomy 32:25; Psalm 94:1; Isaiah 63:4; Romans 12:19; Hebrews 10:30). Vengeance is not human business. Now it may trouble us that this God is concerned with vengeance. But we may begin with the awareness that the assignment of vengeance to God means an end to human vengeance. It is a liberating assertion that I do not need to trouble myself with retaliation, for that is left safely in God's hands. The Psalmist seems to know that. The venomous words show that the reality of vengeance is present. But that these words are addressed to God shows a recognition that this is God's business and not ours. That is the first and most important thing to say about God's vengeance. To affirm that vengeance belongs to God is an act of profound faith. Conversely, to try to keep some vengeance for self and to withhold it from God is to mistrust God, as though we could do it better than God. Affirmation of God's vengeance is in fact a yielding.

2. The vengeance of God is understood as the other side of his compassion—the sovereign redress of a wrong. That

is, in the Old Testament, two motifs belong together. God cannot act to liberate "his" people without at the same time judging and punishing the oppressors who have perverted a just ordering of life. Vengeance by God is not understood as an end in itself. It is discerned as necessary to the establishment and preservation of a just rule. It is a way God "right-wises" life. Thus Deuteronomy 32:35 speaks of vengeance. But this is linked in v. 36 with vindication and compassion for "his" servants:

> Vengeance belongs to me, and requital,
>> for the time when their foot shall slip;
> for the day of their calamity is at hand,
>> and their doom comes swiftly.
> For Yahweh will vindicate his people
>> and have compassion on his servants,
> when he sees that their power is gone,
>> and none remain—bond or free.
> (Deuteronomy 32:35–36)

Such a juxtaposition expresses political realism. When things are shifted on behalf of someone, it means a painful loss for someone else who has encroached on the claims of the first party. Such a juxtaposition may also reflect some childishness. When we are hurt, we do not feel the situation completely righted by compassion unless the offender is also dealt with. This understanding does not eliminate all the theological problems, but it is helpful to see that vengeance is the dark side, perhaps the inevitably dark side, of the mercy of God. Thus:

> . . . to him who smote the first-born of Egypt,
>> for his steadfast love endures forever . . .
> to him who smote great kings,
>> for his steadfast love endures forever. (Psalm 136:10, 17)

The killing of the first-born does not sound like "steadfast love," and it was not so perceived by any Egyptian. But that is steadfast love if one is an Israelite. And such an action is necessary to liberate, though from another perspective, it is simply ruthless vengeance.

3. That God practices vengeance is one way the Bible has of speaking about moral coherence and moral order in which God is actively engaged. The God of the Bible is never neutral, objective, indifferent, or simply balancing things. The world is not on its own. There is an accountability to the purposes of God to which all must answer. God who saves and creates watches over "his" will and judges those who violate "his" purposes. Thus the God who keeps loyalty for thousands is also the one who visits iniquities to the fourth generation (Exodus 34:6–7). And "his" judgment is especially turned against the "wicked," i.e., those who do not serve "his" sovereign purpose (see Psalms 58:10; 149:7). The passionate appeal for faithfulness in Hebrews 10 ends with such an affirmation:

> For we know him who said, "Vengeance is mine,
> I will repay." And again, "The Lord will judge his
> people." It is a fearful thing to fall into the hands of
> the living God." (Hebrews 10:30–31)

Such heavy imagery may not suit our tastes. But it is the imagery found most compelling in terms of urgency in the Church (see Luke 21:22). It may surprise some to note these anticipations of vengeance even in the New Testament.

4. The reality of juxtaposition (vengeance is the back side of compassion) and the assurance of moral coherence in which God has a stake (that is, God takes human action seriously in terms of "his" purpose) leads to the affirmation that God has taken sides in history and acts effectively on behalf of "his" special partners. In the beginning, that special partner is Israel. And so "his" compassion is for Israel, "his" vengeance is against the enemies of Israel. And that is why there is the balance of the rescue of Israel and the destruction of others, as in Psalm 136:10, 15, 17–20. But Israel never becomes the possessor of God's compassion, nor the manager of God's vengeance. Both belong peculiarly to God. God alone exercises them in "his" sovereign freedom and for the sake of that sovereign freedom. When Job's friends, for example, imagine they can "administer" God's compassion, they are dismissed as "foolish."

Thus, in the long run the benefactor of God's compassion/vengeance is not Israel in any mechanical way. Rather, God's action is taken (a) on behalf of the faithful (i.e., righteous, obedient), those who keep Torah:

> The righteous one will rejoice when he sees vengeance;
>> he will bathe his feet in the blood of the wicked one.
> A human ['*adam*] will say, "Surely there is a reward for the
>> righteous one;
>> surely there is a God who rules in the land."
> (Psalm 58:10–11; see also Exodus 34:6)

And God's action is taken (b) on behalf of the poor and needy who are objects of "his" special concern:

> Say to those who are of a fearful heart,
>> "Be strong, fear not!
> Behold our God will come with vengeance,
>> with the recompense of God.
> He will come and save you.
> Then the eyes of the blind shall be opened,
>> and the ears of the deaf unstopped;
> Then shall the lame man leap like a hart,
>> and the tongue of the dumb sing for joy."
> (Isaiah 35:4–6)

> . . . to bring good tidings to the afflicted,
>> to proclaim liberty to the captives. . . .
> to proclaim the year of the Lord's favor,
>> and the day of vengeance of our God. . . .
> (Isaiah 61:1–2)

> O Lord, thou God of vengeance,
>> thou God of vengeance, shine forth!
> O Lord, how long shall the wicked,
>> how long shall the wicked exult? . . .
> They slay the widow and the sojourner,
>> and murder the fatherless.
> (Psalms 94:1, 3, 6; compare 9:18; 12:5–7; 34:6; 35:10)

It is evident that this motif of vengeance for the poor is carried into the New Testament, especially in the gospel of Luke. It is articulated in the song of Mary (Luke 1:51–53) and in the inaugural presentation of Jesus (Luke 4:18–19, which quotes Isaiah 62:1–2). The day of God's vengeance is the day of reversals for the poor and against the unjust rich.[7]

The vengeance of God is not indiscriminate anger. It is a reflection of God's zeal for "his" purposes of justice and freedom. God will not quit until "he" has "his" way, which is at odds with the ways of the world (see Isaiah 55:6–9). And when God's way is thwarted, say the Psalms, God powerfully intervenes—that is, the God with whom we have to do in this practice of psalmic spirituality.

There is no doubt that many of the uses of the vengeance motif in the Psalms are a mixture of good theology and self-interested plea. The speaker identifies himself/herself as one of the faithful deserving poor who has a right to expect and insist upon God's compassionate/vengeful intervention (see Psalms 40:17; 69:29).

This is most poignantly expressed in the "confessions" of Jeremiah. Jeremiah regards himself as undoubtedly one of the faithful poor who asks for compassion which must come as vengeance (see Jeremiah 11:20; 20:12). With Jeremiah, as with the Psalmists and with us, there are no disinterested pray-ers. But the Psalmists are bold to see an appropriate linkage between God's primal commitment and our situation of need. God's commitment is invoked because of a situation of distress that God does not will. And so God is summoned to intervene and to invert the situation. It is that appropriate linkage which is expressed in these Psalms. Such prayer is of-

7. On the theme of "reversal of fortune," see Gottwald, *The Tribes of Yahweh*, 534–40. His focus is on the Song of Hannah. And that in turn is reflected in the Magnificat of Mary. Gottwald is especially attentive to the way in which reversal, which is a literary-rhetorical event, may be evocative of a political-economic reversal.

fered but not because of reasoned conclusion. Rather, in the hurt, anger, and shame, the point of contact is on the one hand the overwhelming need and, on the other, the awareness that Yahweh, God of Israel, is all we have. In that moment of need, Israel's God is the last, best hope of the believing community. And so Israel must seek rectification, and that requires forceful action.[8]

Vengeance and Compassion

Having said all of that, we may note that this settlement of the question of vengeance is provisional. The most sensitive poets of Israel are troubled about this way of thinking. And at peak moments of literary insight and theological imagination, they know God to be troubled too.

In the Old Testament, we may cite two texts, parallel in structure, which disclose the struggle in the heart of God. In the flood narrative, the beginning in Genesis 6:5–7 has God resolve to take vengeance on "his" wayward creation:

> Yahweh saw that the wickedness of the human [*ha-'adam*] was great in the earth, and that every imagination of the thoughts of his heart was only evil continually. And Yahweh repented that he had made the human [*ha-'adam*] on the earth, and it

8. Mendenhall has provided an especially helpful discussion of vengeance (*The Tenth Generation,* chapter 3). It is his argument that vengeance is a political idea and ought not to be understood as a raw, primitive seeking of retaliation. Rather, it is the maintenance of political order and sovereignty in an established "imperium." The responsible Lord intervenes to right situations which have departed from the over-all governing pattern. Thus vengeance is both punishment and vindication in Israel. While I have not followed Mendenhall precisely, his essay is especially suggestive.

> grieved him to his heart. So Yahweh said, "I will
> blot out the human [*ha-'adam*] whom I have created
> from the face of the ground [*ha-'adamah*], human
> ['*adam*] and beast and creeping things and birds of
> the air, for I am sorry that I have made them."

But note that God makes the resolve not in anger, but in grief
and sorrow. The flood narrative spins out the troubled tale.
But by Genesis 8:21, something decisive has happened. Nothing is changed in the imagination of humankind, which is
still evil:

> Yahweh said in his heart, "I will never again curse
> the ground [*ha-'adamah*] because of the human
> [*ha-'adam*], for the imagination of the human's
> [*ha-'adam*] heart is evil from his youth; neither will
> I ever again destroy every living creature as I have
> done.

What has happened is a change wrought in the heart of God,
who will no longer take vengeance. The move in God's heart
from 6:5–7 to 8:21 suggests that instead of humankind suffering, God takes the suffering as "his" own. God resolves to
turn the grief in on "himself" rather than to rage against "his"
creation. God bears the vengeance of God in order that "his"
creation can have compassion.

The same "turn" is more visible in Hosea 11:1–9. Verses
1–7 are a conventional statement of God's anger and punishment. But in vv. 8–9, God has internalized the rage, turned
the anger so that "his" own "heart quakes." God resolves not
to take vengeance on Israel, but to contain it within "his" own
person:

How can I give you up, O Ephraim?
>How can I surrender you, O Israel?
How can I make you like Admah?
>How can I treat you like Zeboiim?
My heart recoils within me,
>my compassion grows warm and tender.
I will not execute my fierce anger,
>I will not again destroy Ephraim;
For I am God and not a man—the Holy One in your midst,
>and I will not come to destroy. (Hosea 11:8–9)

In this profound moment, God breaks with the habits of heaven and earth. God presents "himself" in radical graciousness. "He" is "God and not man." This God is also a God unlike any of the other gods (see Psalm 82). Such graciousness is not easy, in heaven or on earth. It is not simply or obviously gained. It is gained only by God's acceptance and internalization of the vengeance which gets outwardly expressed, now, only as compassion. Unmitigated compassion is possible only because God bears the pain of vengeance in "his" own person.

A Way Through Vengeance

Finally, we must ask, how does Christian faith assess these statements about the vengeance of God? How are these themes taken up in the New Testament? There is ground for saying that the New Testament discloses God as having moved from vengeance to compassion. But that argument must be articulated very delicately:

1. We must not pretend that the New Testament gives a "higher" view of God in contrast to the Old Testament. Such

an evolutionary notion misreads the evidence. In both Testaments, we have to do with the same God.

2. We have seen that the Old Testament already knows about the problem in the experience of God's vengeance. Israel already understands that the grief of God moves beyond vengeance. In addition to Genesis 6:5–7; 8:20–22; and Hosea 11:8–9 (which we have quoted), see also Psalms 103:6–14; and 130.

3. We have seen that the New Testament still makes important use of the motif of God's vengeance. In the New Testament, this God has not become a romantic who has no passion for "his" purposes. This God still holds to "his" jealous sovereignty and intervenes for the sake of it. There is no way around the hard sayings in the New Testament.

4. But, finally, we come to those staggering ethical injunctions about love in the place of vengeance:

> You have heard that it was said, "You shall love your neighbor and hate your enemy." But I say to you, love your enemies and pray for those who persecute you, so that you may be sons of your Father who is in heaven; for he makes his sun rise on the evil and on the good, and he sends rain on the just and the unjust. . . . You, therefore, must be perfect, as your heavenly Father is perfect. (Matthew 5:43–45, 48)

> Bless those who persecute you; bless and do not curse them. . . . Beloved, never avenge yourselves, but leave it to the wrath of God, for it is written, "Vengeance is mine, I will repay, says the Lord." . . . Do not be overcome by evil, but overcome evil with good. (Romans 12:14, 19)

This is the most extreme claim made in this regard. But notice, these ethical statements are in fact theological claims. What we are to do relates to who God is: "Be perfect, as your heavenly Father is perfect." The possibility of a vengeance-free ethic is rooted in the staggering reality of God. And so we are driven to the crucifixion, in which God has decisively dealt with the reality of evil which must be judged. God has responded with "his" own powerful inclination for justice. There is no less of vengeance in the New Testament. But God has wrought it in "his" own person, and so the world has been purged and grace has overcome.

For those who are troubled about the Psalms of vengeance, there is a way beyond them. But it is not an easy or "natural way." It is not the way of careless religious goodwill. It is not the way of moral indifference or flippancy. It is, rather, the way of crucifixion, of accepting the rage and grief and terror of evil in ourselves in order to be liberated for compassion toward others. In the gospel, Christians know "a more excellent way" (1 Corinthians 12:31). But it is not the first way:

> Jesus' Third Way is not a law but a gift. It establishes us in freedom, not necessity. It is something we are not required to do, but enabled to do. It is a "Thou mayest," not a "Thou must." It is not something we do in order to secure our own righteousness before God. It is rather something that we are made capable of when we know that the power of God is greater than the powers of death.[9]

My hunch is that there is a way beyond the Psalms of vengeance, but it is a way through them and not around them. And that is so because of what in fact goes on with us. Willy-

9. Wink, *Jesus and Nonviolence,* 82.

nilly, we are vengeful creatures. Thus these harsh Psalms must be fully embraced as our own. Our rage and indignation must be fully owned and fully expressed. And then (only then) can our rage and indignation be yielded to the mercy of God. In taking this route through them, we take the route God "himself" has gone. We are not permitted a cheaper, easier, more "enlightened" way.[10]

10. Marie Augusta Neal discusses the need for "relinquishment" of an economic kind (*A Socio-Theology of Letting Go*). To be viable such economic relinquishment must be matched by linguistic, liturgical, emotional "letting go."

Bibliography

1. Works Cited

Anderson, Bernhard W. *Out of the Depths: The Psalms Speak for Us Today.*
1st ed. Philadelphia: Westminster, 1974.
———, and Steven Bishop. *Out of the Depths: The Psalms Speak for Us
Today.* 3d ed. Louisville: Westminster John Knox, 2000.
Barth, Karl. *Church Dogmatics.* IV.2: *The Doctrine of Reconciliation.*
Translated by Geoffrey Bromiley. Edinburgh: T. & T. Clark, 1958.
Battles, Ford Lewis, translator and editor. *The Piety of John Calvin: An
Anthology Illustrative of the Spirituality of the Reformer.* Grand Rapids:
Baker, 1978.
Becker, Ernst. *The Denial of Death.* New York: Free Press, 1973.
Berger, Peter L. *A Rumor of Angels: Modern Society and the Rediscovery of
the Supernatural.* Garden City, NY: Doubleday, 1969.
———. *A Rumor of Angels: Modern Society and the Rediscovery of the
Supernatural.* Expanded ed. New York: Anchor, 1990.
Book of Common Prayer. New York: Seabury, 1979.
Brueggemann, Walter. "The Formfulness of Grief." *Interpretation* 31
(1977) 263–75. Reprinted in *The Psalms and the Life of Faith,* edited
by Patrick D. Miller, 84–97. Minneapolis: Fortress, 1995.
———. "Psalms and the Life of Faith: A Suggested Typology of Function."
Journal for the Study of the Old Testament 17 (1980) 3–32. Reprinted
in *The Psalms and the Life of Faith,* edited by Patrick D. Miller.
Minneapolis: Fortress, 1995.
———. *Theology of the Old Testament: Testimony, Dispute, Advocacy.*
Minneapolis: Fortress, 1997.
Buber, Martin. *I and Thou.* Translated by Walter Kaufmann. New York:
Scribner, 1970.
Calvin, John. *A Commentary on the Psalms.* Translated by Arthur Golding.
Revised and edited by T. H. L. Parker. London: James Clarke, 1965.
Gerstenberger, Erhard S. "Der klagende Mensch: Anmerkungen zu den
Klagegattungen in Israel." In *Probleme biblischer Theologie: Gerhard*

von Rad zum 70. Geburtstag, edited by Hans Walter Wolff, 64–72. Munich: Kaiser, 1971.

———. "Life Situations and Theological Concepts of Old Testament Psalms." *Old Testament Essays* 18 (2005) 82–92.

———. *Theologies in the Old Testament.* Translated by John Bowden. Minneapolis: Fortress, 2002.

———, and Wolfgang Schrage. *Suffering.* Translated by John E. Steely. Biblical Encounters Series. Nashville: Abingdon, 1980.

Gilkey, Langdon. *Naming the Whirlwind: The Renewal of God-Language.* Indianapolis: Bobbs-Merrill, 1969.

Gottwald, Norman K. *The Tribes of Yahweh: A Sociology of the Religion of Liberated Israel, 1250–1050 B.C.E.* Maryknoll, NY: Orbis, 1979.

Gunkel, Hermann. *An Introduction to the Psalms.* Translated by James D. Nogalski. Mercer Library of Biblical Studies. Macon, GA: Mercer University Press, 1998.

Guthrie, Harvey H. Jr. *Israel's Sacred Songs: A Study of Dominant Themes.* New York: Seabury, 1966.

———. *Theology as Thanksgiving: From Israel's Psalms to the Church's Eucharist.* New York: Seabury, 1981.

Laing, R. D. *The Politics of Experience.* New York: Pantheon, 1967.

Mendenhall, George E. *The Tenth Generation: The Origins of the Biblical Tradition.* Baltimore: John Hopkins University Press, 1973.

Mowinckel, Sigmund. *The Psalms and Israel's Worship.* Translated by D. R. Ap-Thomas. 2 vols. in 1. 1962. Reprinted, Biblical Resource Series. Forward by James L. Crenshaw. Grand Rapids, Eerdmans, 2004.

Mumford, Lewis. *The Myth of the Machine.* 2 vols. New York: Harcourt Brace and World, 1966, 1967.

Neal, Marie Augusta. *A Socio-Theology of Letting Go: The Role of a First World Church Facing Third World Peoples.* New York: Paulist, 1977.

Ricoeur, Paul. *Freud and Philosophy: An Essay on Interpretation.* Translated by Denis Savage. New Haven: Yale University Press, 1970.

———. "Biblical Hermeneutics." *Semeia* 4 (1975) 108–35.

Terrien, Samuel. *The Elusive Presence: Toward a New Biblical Theology.* 1978. Reprinted, Eugene, OR: Wipf & Stock, 2000.

Tournier, Paul. *A Place for You: Psychology and Religion.* Translated by Edwin Hudson. New York: Harper & Row, 1968.

Troeger, Thomas H. *Rage! Reflect, Rejoice! Praying with the Psalmists.* Philadelphia: Westminster, 1977.

Westermann, Claus. "Creation and History in the Old Testament." In *The Gospel and Human Destiny,* edited by Vilmos Vajta, 11–38. The Gospel Encounters History Series. Minneapolis: Augsburg, 1971.

―――. *The Psalms: Structure, Content and Message.* Translated by Ralph D. Gehrke. Minneapolis: Augsburg, 1980.

―――. *What Does the Old Testament Say about God?* Translated by Friedemann Golka. Atlanta: John Knox, 1979.

Wiesel, Elie. *Memoirs: All Rivers Run to the Sea.* New York: Knopf, 1995.

Wink, Walter. *Jesus and Nonviolence: A Third Way.* Facets. Minneapolis: Fortress, 2003.

Zenger, Erich. *A God of Vengeance? Understanding the Psalms of Divine Wrath* Translated by Linda M. Maloney. Louisville: Westminster John Knox, 1996.

2. Additional Works on the Psalms

Arackal, Joseph J., translator. *The Psalms in Inclusive Language.* Collegeville, MN: Liturgical, 1993.

Bland, Dave, and David Fleer, editors. *Performing the Psalms.* St. Louis. Chalice, 2005.

Brown, William P. *Seeing the Psalms: A Theology of Metaphor.* Louisville: Westminster John Knox, 2002.

Brueggemann, Walter. *Abiding Astonishment: Psalms, Modernity, and the Making of History.* Literary Currents in Biblical Interpretation. Louisville: Westminster John Knox, 1991.

―――. *Israel's Praise: Doxology against Idolatry and Ideology.* Philadelphia: Fortress, 1988.

―――. *The Message of the Psalms: A Theological Commentary.* Minneapolis: Augsburg, 1984.

―――. *The Psalms and the Life of Faith.* Edited by Patrick D. Miller. Minneapolis: Fortress, 1995.

―――. *Spirituality of the Psalms.* Facets. Minneapolis: Fortress, 2002.

Clifford, Richard J. *Psalms.* 2 vols. Abingdon Old Testament Commentaries. Nashville: Abingdon, 2002–2003.

DeClaissé-Walford, Nancy L. *Introduction to the Psalms: A Song from Ancient Israel.* St. Louis: Chalice, 2004.

Eaton, John. *The Psalms: A Historical and Spiritual Commentary with an Introduction and New Translation.* London: T. & T. Clark, 2003.

Holladay, William L. *The Psalms through Three Thousand Years: Prayerbook of a Cloud of Witnesses.* Minneapolis: Fortress, 1993.

Hopkins, Denise Dombkowski. *Journey through the Psalms.* Rev. ed. St. Louis: Chalice, 2002.

Jaki, Stanley L. *Praying the Psalms: A Commentary.* Grand Rapids: Eerdmans, 2001.

Lewis, Thomas Griffith. *Finding God: Praying the Psalms in Times of Depression.* Louisville: Westminster John Knox, 2002.

Limburg, James. *Psalms.* Westminster Bible Companion. Louisville: Westminster John Knox, 2000.

———. *Psalms for Sojourners.* 2d ed. Minneapolis: Fortress, 2002.

Mays, James Luther. *The Lord Reigns: A Theological Handbook to the Psalms.* Interpretation. Louisville: Westminster John Knox, 1994.

———. *Preaching and Teaching the Psalms.* Edited by Patrick D. Miller and Gene M. Tucker. Louisville: Westminster John Knox, 2006.

McCann, J. Clinton Jr., and James C. Howell. *Preaching the Psalms.* Nashville: Abingdon, 2001.

Miller, Patrick D. *Interpreting the Psalms.* Philadelphia: Fortress, 1986.

———. *They Cried to the Lord: The Form and Theology of Biblical Prayer.* Minneapolis: Fortress, 1994.

Parrish, V. Steven. *A Story of the Psalms: Conversation, Canon, and Congregation.* Collegeville, MN: Liturgical, 2003.

Paulsell, William O. *Let My Prayer Rise to God: A Spirituality for Praying the Psalms.* St. Louis: Chalice, 2002.

Pleins, J. David. *The Psalms: Songs of Tragedy, Hope, and Justice.* Bible and Liberation Series. Maryknoll, NY: Orbis, 1993.

Reid, Stephen Breck, *Listening In: A Multicultural Reading of the Psalms.* Nashville: Abingdon, 1997.

———. editor. *Psalms and Practice: Worship, Virtue, and Authority.* Collegeville, MN: Liturgical, 2001.

Steussy, Marti J. *Psalms.* Chalice Commentaries for Today. St. Louis: Chalice, 2004.

Swenson, Kristin M. *Living through Pain: Psalms and the Search for Wholeness.* Waco, TX: Baylor University Press, 2005.

Wallace, Howard N. *Words to God, Word from God: The Psalms in the Prayer and Preaching of the Church.* Burlington, VT: Ashgate, 2005.

Westermann, Claus. *Praise and Lament in the Psalms.* Translated by K. R. Crim and R. N. Soulen. Atlanta: John Knox, 1981.

Wieder, Laurance, editor. *The Poets' Book of Psalms: The Complete Psalter as Rendered by Twenty-five Poets from the Sixteenth to the Twentieth Centuries.* San Francisco: HarperSanFrancisco, 1995.

3. Additional Works by Walter Brueggemann

Awed to Heaven, Rooted in Earth: Prayers of Walter Brueggemann. Minneapolis: Fortress, 2003.

The Bible Makes Sense. Rev. ed. Louisville: Westminster John Knox, 2001.

Biblical Perspectives on Evangelism: Living in a Three-Storied Universe. Nashville: Abingdon, 1993.

The Book that Breathes New Life: Scriptural Authority and Biblical Theology. Minneapolis: Fortress, 2005.

Cadences of Home: Preaching among Exiles. Louisville: Westminster John Knox, 1997.

A Commentary on Jeremiah: Exile and Homecoming. Grand Rapids: Eerdmans, 1998.

The Covenanted Self: Explorations in Law and Covenant. Minneapolis: Fortress, 1999.

The Creative Word: Canon as Model for Biblical Education. Philadelphia: Fortress, 1982.

David's Truth in Israel's Imagination and Memory. 2d ed. Minneapolis: Fortress, 2002.

Deep Memory, Exuberant Hope: Contested Truth in a Post-Christian World. Minneapolis: Fortress, 2000.

Deuteronomy. Abingdon Old Testament Commentaries. Nashville: Abingdon, 2001.

Finally Comes the Poet: Daring Speech for Proclamation. Minneapolis: Fortress, 1989.

1 & 2 Kings. Smyth & Helwys Bible Commentary. Macon, GA: Smyth & Helwys, 2000.

First and Second Samuel. Interpretation. Louisville: Westminster John Knox, 1990.

Genesis. Interpretation. Atlanta: John Knox, 1982.

Hope within History. Atlanta: John Knox, 1987.

Hopeful Imagination: Prophetic Voices in Exile. Philadelphia: Fortress, 1986.

Ichabod toward Home: The Journey of God's Glory. 2002. Reprinted, Eugene, OR: Wipf & Stock, 2005.

In Man We Trust: The Neglected Side of Biblical Faith. 1972. Reprinted, Eugene, OR: Wipf & Stock, 2006.

Inscribing the Text: Sermons and Prayers of Walter Brueggemann. Minneapolis: Fortress, 2004.

Interpretation and Obedience: From Faithful Reading to Faithful Living. Minneapolis: Fortress, 1991.

An Introduction to the Old Testament: The Canon and Christian Imagination. Louisville: Westminster John Knox, 2003.

Isaiah. Westminster Bible Companion. Louisville: Westminster John Knox, 1998.

Israel's Praise: Doxology against Idolatry and Ideology. Philadelphia: Fortress, 1988.

The Land: Place as Gift, Promise, and Challenge in Biblical Faith. 2d ed. Minneapolis: Fortress, 2002.

Like Fire in the Bones: Listening for the Prophetic Word in Jeremiah. Minneapolis: Fortress, 2006.

Old Testament Theology: Essays on Structure, Theme, and Text. Minneapolis: Fortress, 1992.

Peace. Understanding Biblical Themes. St. Louis: Chalice, 2001.

Power, Providence, and Personality: Biblical Insight into Life and Ministry. Louisville: Westminster John Knox, 1990.

The Prophetic Imagination. 2d ed. Minneapolis: Fortress, 2001.

Revelation and Violence: A Study of Contextualization. Milwaukee: Marquette University Press, 1986.

Reverberations of Faith: A Theological Handbook of Old Testament Themes. Louisville: Westminster John Knox, 2002.

A Social Reading of the Old Testament: Prophetic Approaches to Israel's Communal Life. Edited by Patrick D. Miller. Minneapolis: Fortress, 1994.

Solomon: Israel's Ironic Icon of Human Achievement. Studies on Personalities of the Old Testament. Columbia, SC: University of South Carolina Press, 2005.

Testimony to Otherwise: The Witness of Elijah and Elisha. St. Louis: Chalice, 2001.

Texts that Linger, Words that Explode: Listening to Prophetic Voices. Edited by Patrick D. Miller. Minneapolis: Fortress, 2000.

Texts under Negotiation: The Bible and Postmodern Imagination. Minneapolis: Fortress, 1993.

Theology of the Old Testament: Testimony, Dispute, Advocacy. Minneapolis: Fortress, 1997.

The Threat of Life: Sermons on Pain, Power, and Weakness. Edited by Charles L. Campbell. Minneapolis: Fortress, 1996.

With Sharon Parks and Thomas Groome. *To Act Justly, Love Tenderly, Walk Humbly: An Agenda for Ministers.* 1986. Reprinted, Eugene, OR: Wipf & Stock, 1997.

Tradition for Crisis: A Study in Hosea. Atlanta: John Knox, 1968.

Using God's Resources Wisely: Isaiah and Urban Possibility. Louisville: Westminster John Knox, 1993.

With Hans Walter Wolff. *The Vitality of Old Testament Traditions.* 2d ed. Atlanta: John Knox, 1982.

The Word that Redescribes the World: The Bible and Discipleship. Edited by
     Patrick D. Miller. Minneapolis: Fortress, 2006.
Worship in Ancient Israel: An Essential Guide. Abingdon Essential Guides.
     Nashville: Abingdon, 2005.

Scripture Index

Subject and Author Index

Made in the USA
Coppell, TX
12 March 2020